Campaign

First Newbury 1643

The turning point

First Newbury 1643

The turning point

Keith Roberts · Illustrated by Graham Turner

Series editor Lee Johnson · Consultant editor David G Chandler

First published in Great Britain in 2003 by Osprey Publishing, Elms Court,
Chapel Way, Botley, Oxford OX2 9LP, United Kingdom.
Email: info@ospreypublishing.com

ISBN 1 84176 333 0

Editor: Lee Johnson
Design: The Black Spot
Index by Alison Worthington
Maps by The Map Studio
3D bird's-eye views by The Black Spot
Battlescene artwork by Graham Turner

Originated by The Electronic Page Company, Cwmbran, UK
Printed in China through World Print Ltd.

03 04 05 06 07   10 9 8 7 6 5 4 3 2 1

FOR A CATALOGUE OF ALL BOOKS PUBLISHED BY OSPREY MILITARY
AND AVIATION PLEASE CONTACT:

Osprey Direct UK, P.O. Box 140,
Wellingborough, Northants, NN8 2FA, UK
E-mail: info@ospreydirect.co.uk

Osprey Direct USA, c/o MBI Publishing,
P.O. Box 1, 729 Prospect Ave, Osceola, WI 54020, USA
E-mail: info@ospreydirectusa.com

www.ospreypublishing.com

Author's note

There are inevitably a number of different spellings of
certain surnames within the text where the author has
followed a contemporary quotation exactly. It should be
pointed out that in this period there were often several
different ways in which an individual's name was commonly
spelt. They may often have spelt their own name a variety
of ways on different documents.

Artist's note

Readers may care to note that the original paintings from
which the colour plates in this book were prepared are
available for private sale. All reproduction copyright
whatsoever is retained by the Publishers. All enquiries
should be addressed to:

Graham Turner
'Five Acres'
Buslins Lane,
Chartridge, Chesham,
Bucks, HP5 2SN
UK

The Publishers regret that they can enter into no
correspondence upon this matter.

KEY TO MILITARY SYMBOLS

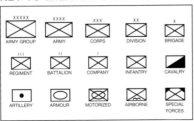

CONTENTS

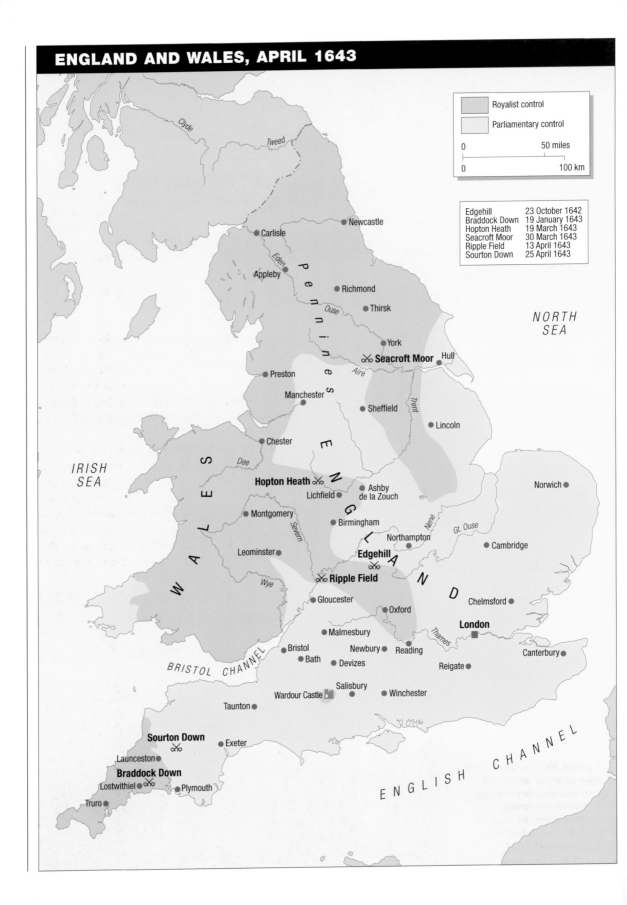

ENGLAND AND WALES, APRIL 1643

Royalist control

Parliamentary control

| 0 | 50 miles |
| 0 | 100 km |

Edgehill	23 October 1642
Braddock Down	19 January 1643
Hopton Heath	19 March 1643
Seacroft Moor	30 March 1643
Ripple Field	13 April 1643
Sourton Down	25 April 1643

Clyde

Tweed

Newcastle

Carlisle

Eden

Appleby

P e n n i n e s

Richmond

Ouse

Thirsk

NORTH SEA

York

⚔ **Seacroft Moor**   Hull

Preston   *Aire*

Manchester

Sheffield

Trent

IRISH SEA

Chester

Dee

E   Lincoln

N

Hopton Heath ⚔   G

Lichfield   Ashby de la Zouch

Montgomery   Birmingham

Severn   L   *Nene*

Northampton   *Gt. Ouse*

Leominster   A   Cambridge

Wye   ⚔ **Ripple Field**   N

Gloucester   D   Chelmsford

Oxford

Edgehill ⚔

W A L E S

Malmesbury   London

Bristol   Newbury   Reading   *Thames*

Bath   Devizes   Canterbury

BRISTOL CHANNEL   Salisbury   Reigate

Wardour Castle 🏰   Winchester

Taunton

Sourton Down ⚔   Exeter

Launceston   ENGLISH CHANNEL

Braddock Down ⚔

Lostwithiel   Plymouth

Truro

INTRODUCTION

'The Enemy had no Army; nor, by all Intelligence, was like to form any soon enough to be able to relieve it [Gloucester]; *and if they had an Army, that it was much better for his Majesty to force them to that distance from London, and to fight there, where he could be supplied with whatsoever he wanted, could choose his own ground, where his brave Body of Horse would be able to Defeat any Army they could raise, than to seek them in their own Quarters.'*

The Earl of Clarendon, a Royalist courtier and author of the *History of the Rebellion*, on the decision to besiege the City of Gloucester.

By August 1643 the Royalist cause was in the ascendant. In the North, Lord Fairfax's Parliament army had been cut to pieces at Adwalton Moor on 30 June. In the West, Sir William Waller's Parliament army had been shattered at Roundway Down on 13 July, and Bristol, the second wealthiest city in England, had surrendered on terms on 26 July following a Royalist assault. On 10 August, the Royalists summoned the City of Gloucester to surrender and expected an easy victory.

Support for the Parliamentary cause had weakened under the pressure of this sequence of Royalist successes. Parliament and its General, the Earl of Essex, now had little option but to make a great attempt to relieve the city of Gloucester, as the fall of one more loyal city would be a great boost for Royalist sympathisers, particularly those in London, and for those who now desired peace at almost any price. The London newsbook *The Parliament Scout* was pessimistic and wrote after the fall of Bristol, 'But is this all? No, we are afraid our Scout will the next week bring the newes either

Sir Edmund Waller's Royalist plot to raise an armed uprising in London was uncovered in May 1643. Two of his closest associates, Nathaniel Tomkins (Waller's brother-in-law) and Richard Challoner, were executed on 5 July 1643.

of the loss of Gloster or Exeter or both.' Apart from the impact on morale if the city fell, Gloucester was also strategically important to the Parliament cause, as it was now the last Parliament stronghold in the West. Control of Gloucester meant control of the resources of the surrounding area, particularly iron ore used for munitions. The city also served as a block on the route between the Royalist headquarters in Oxford and Wales, which was an increasingly important source of support for the Royalist cause. An active garrison at Gloucester would, furthermore, require the Royalists to maintain strong garrisons in order to defend and maintain control over their own territory, and this would divert soldiers to garrison duty who were needed as reinforcements for the main Royalist field army.

When the Earl of Essex marched out on his expedition to relieve the siege of Gloucester he knew that the future of the Parliament cause hung in the balance.

COURSE OF THE WAR 1642–43

At the outbreak of the Civil War the main armies raised by each side had been concentrated for a campaign that culminated with the indecisive battle of Edgehill (Campaign Series No. 82, *Edgehill 1642*). After Edgehill King Charles and his army marched to Oxford, and from there through Reading to London. Essex's Parliamentary army took a more direct route through Daventry and St Albans arriving at London on 7 November, two days before the leading elements of the King's army.

Essex had established several advanced posts to protect London at Kingston, Acton and Brentford. On 12 November, Prince Rupert, the King's nephew and the Royalist cavalry commander, led the attack and the two Parliament regiments at Brentford were beaten out of the town with severe losses. The main impact of Prince Rupert's attack was to increase the fears of London citizens that the King's army would plunder the city if the Royalists overwhelmed Essex's army. It was this fear that caused Londoners to muster at a full strength of 8,000 infantry when the city authorities called out the London Trained Bands to join the Earl of Essex's army at Turnham Green. With this reinforcement Essex had nearly 24,000 men to oppose the King's army. Outnumbered and short of ammunition, the Royalists retired to Oxford to reconsider their strategy as it was now clear that the war would not be over by Christmas. London, the centre of the Parliament cause, could not be taken by direct assault. The campaigning season for 1642 was over and both armies went into Winter quarters, the Royalists in the towns and villages around Oxford and the Parliament army around London.

Both sides had expected an early conclusion to the war, either through negotiation or a quick battlefield victory for one side or the other. Consequently both sides had concentrated most of the soldiers their supporters had raised into two opposing field armies. After Edgehill and Turnham Green it was evident that the war would not be over quickly. Both sides then sought to dominate the territories from which they could draw resources (money, recruits and war material) to support their campaigns, the ports through which arms and men could be imported and key strategic points that could protect communication routes for the movement of recruits, arms and ammunition. Most Englishmen who were

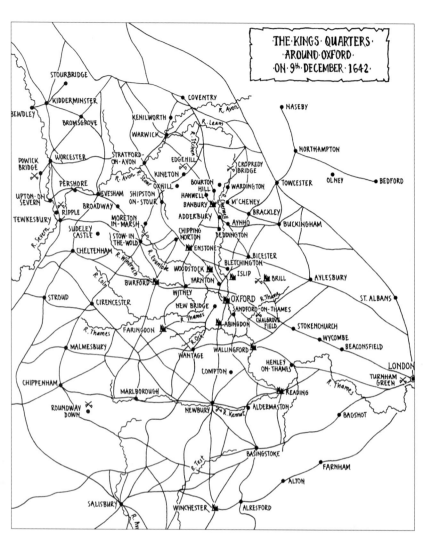

Royalist Garrisons of the King's Oxford Army, 9 December 1642. *Oxford*: Four infantry regiments (The King's Lifeguard, Colonel Charles Gerard's, Sir William Pennyman's and Sir Ralph Dutton's), Three cavalry troops (Lifeguard and Gentleman Pensioners). *Reading*: Six infantry regiments (Colonel Richard Feilding's Tertia consisting of his own, Colonel Richard Bolle's, Sir Thomas Salusbury's and Colonel Edward Stradling's and two other regiments, Colonel Henry Lunsford's and Sir Edward Fitton's), Two cavalry regiments (Sir Arthur Aston's and Sir Thomas Aston's). *Wallingford*: Two infantry regiments (Colonel Thomas Blagge's and Earl Rivers'), One cavalry regiment (Lord Digby's). *Abingdon*: One infantry regiment (Sir Lewis Dyve's), Two cavalry regiments (Prince Rupert's and Lord Wilmot's). *Farringdon*: One cavalry regiment (Prince Maurice's), Two dragoon regiments (Colonel Sir Edward Duncombe's and Colonel Edward Grey's). *Winchester*: One cavalry regiment (Lord Grandison's). *Burford*: One cavalry regiment (Sir John Byron's), One dragoon regiment (Colonel James Usher's). *Brill*: Two regiments of infantry (Sir Gilbert Gerard's and Lord Molineux's). *Banbury*: Two regiments of infantry (The Earl of Northampton's and Colonel John Belasyse's), One regiment of cavalry (Prince of Wales'). *Woodstock*: One regiment of infantry (The Lord General's), One troop of cavalry (the Lord General's). *Eynsham*: One regiment of cavalry (The Earl of Carnarvon's). *Islip*: One regiment of cavalry (Lord Andover's).

strongly committed to one side or the other had joined the main Royalist or Parliament field armies. Now a number of men with local influence in their county returned home and attempted to establish control for their party.

Some supporters of each side had never left their homes and there had been some military activity in the counties, with cities and towns actively held for one side or the other, and some local troops had been raised. However, defensive measures were also taken in many cities, towns and country estates by people who simply sought to defend themselves in an uncertain world. Most of those who had stayed at home rather than join one army or the other hoped to avoid becoming involved in the war at all. Englishmen and women were all too aware of the consequences of warfare on civilians, courtesy of accounts in pamphlets that were published complete with horrifying illustrations of the rape, torture and murder of civilians during the Thirty Years War in Germany (1618–48) and the rebellion in Ireland (1641–53). Efforts were made in several counties during the winter of 1642/43 to agree some form of neutrality pact to keep out of the war altogether. Pacts could be anything from an aggressive agreement to defend the county against all comers or simply a local truce.

The cornet (cavalry flag) of Colonel Sir Richard Grenville when he was in Parliament service. The motto 'England Bleeding' illustrates the perspective of many Englishmen over the Civil War. Grenville turned coat and joined the Royalists in March 1644. (Dr Williams Library).

Edward Somerset, Lord Herbert, was appointed second in command to the Marquis of Hertford because of his wealth and influence in South Wales. He was able to recruit substantial numbers of Welshmen for the Royalist cause.

One of the more interesting examples was the truce agreed in late February 1643 between Royalists in Cornwall and Parliament supporters in Devon. The agreement also set out arrangements for a conference to be held at Exeter with the intention of combining the counties of Cornwall, Devon, Somerset and Dorset in a neutral association. In the end these efforts at neutrality came to nothing, as neither the Royalists nor Parliament could accept parts of the country opting out of the war and each took steps to suppress neutrals, or 'neuters' as they were known. Both sides assigned particular commanders to control particular counties, but the creation of a series of four associations by the Parliament may have tapped more successfully into the desire of many counties and their inhabitants for self-defence. These four associations were the Midlands Association (15 December 1642), the Western Association (11 February 1643), the Southern Association (4 November 1643) and, most successful of all, the Eastern Association (20 December 1642).

Some of the new armies raised in the counties had an ephemeral existence, such as Edward Somerset, Lord Herbert's 'mushrump' (mushroom) army – so-called because it was raised and destroyed in a short space of time. Others soon began to have an impact on the conduct of the war outside their local quarrels, particularly those in the North and in the West Country.

The War in the Centre

Although the main Royalist field army was settled in its winter quarters in the City of Oxford and a ring of fortified places surrounding it [see map on page 9], Prince Rupert was soon active in a series of raids against Parliament towns. The Earl of Essex had a more ambitious plan for the start of a new campaigning season, and he made his move while Prince Rupert and his cavalry were occupied in the Midlands. Essex intended to take Reading, the strongest of the Royalist fortified points surrounding Oxford. It was a town whose inhabitants were 'very willing and forward to the endangering of both their lives and fortunes' to assist parliamentary forces. Essex had good intelligence from sympathisers in Reading and he was probably well aware of the decision by the Royalist council of war at Oxford to instruct the garrison commander, Sir Arthur Aston, to 'draw off his garrison to the King' so as to increase the Royalist marching army. The Royalists believed that they had until the end of April to effect a withdrawal as 'before which time it was conceived the enemy would not adventure to take the field'. Most armies at this period did not start campaigning until the spring, partly because prolonged exposure to harsh weather would cause losses though disease, but mainly because the grass had begun to grow by then. An army needed growing grass to provide the bulk of the fodder required for cavalry mounts and for the horses it relied upon to draw its supply trains.

Essex made his move much earlier than the Royalists expected, bringing together a force to besiege Reading consisting of his own soldiers reinforced by troops raised in the eastern counties by William Lord Grey of Wark and a contingent from the garrison at Aylesbury. In his approach march Essex demonstrated his military expertise by deceiving his opponents with a feint. It was a tactic that would serve him well later in the year as he began his return march from Gloucester. Essex summoned the town of Reading to surrender on 15 April and received a robust response from the Royalist governor, Sir Arthur Aston, to the effect that 'he would not deliver the town until wheat was forty shillings a bushel, and as for the women and children they should dye with him'. Aston was a competent soldier but was disliked by almost everyone who knew him. Clarendon's thumbnail sketch recorded that Aston 'had the fortune to be very much esteemed where he was not known, and very much detested where he was'. At first sight, the siege of Reading might appear to be siege warfare in the Dutch style, with the objective of breaking the ring of strong-points around the Royalist capital of Oxford. However, Essex knew the garrison would be withdrawn soon, and his objective was to capture or kill a significant proportion of the Royalist field army and to take control of the gunpowder supplies in the magazine, the Royalists' largest single supply of gunpowder outside Oxford. Essex's response to an offer to surrender the town on condition the garrison could march away with its baggage was: 'we came for the men, not the town'. However, after a relief force under the Royalist Lord General the Earl of Forth and Prince Rupert was beaten off at Caversham Bridge, Reading surrendered on terms. With a Royalist relief force still nearby, Essex allowed the garrison generous terms and they marched out to rejoin the main Royalist field army with 'four peeces of ordnance'. They left behind most of the artillery deployed in the town's defences and 28 barrels of gunpowder.

Possession of Reading gave Essex the option of making an advance on Oxford itself, but at this point the campaign ground to a halt because an outbreak of disease, probably typhus, decimated his army. The Royalists were no better off, as the Reading garrison was also infected and brought the disease with them when they joined the main Royalist field army in its quarters at Culham camp near Abingdon.

Prince Rupert continued to mount raids on outlying Parliament quarters and convoys. On his return from an unsuccessful raid seeking a Parliament pay convoy he was intercepted by Parliament cavalry at Chalgrove Field (18 June 1643). The Royalists brushed past the Parliament cavalry, and the MP John Hampden (one of the five members of Parliament Charles I had famously failed to arrest in the House of Commons) was mortally wounded in the skirmish.

The War in the North

In the North of England the Earl of Newcastle and his field commander, James King, had raised troops to secure Newcastle upon Tyne for a landing by Queen Henrietta Maria and the shipment of arms and gunpowder she had purchased in Holland, the centre of the international arms trade. Newcastle's troops would escort the arms, and the Queen herself to join the main Royalist army in the south. To secure the route south, Newcastle sent Sir John Henderson to occupy Newark, where the Great North Road crosses the River Trent, and waited for the Queen's arrival. The ships that carried Queen Henrietta Maria's arms shipment could not reach the Tyne but she was able to land at Bridlington on 22 February 1643. Newcastle's troops reached Bridlington two days later, and on 7 March the Queen and her arms shipment were escorted into York. Newcastle's military activity had been restricted while he awaited the arrival of the Queen. He now had the choice 'whether to march with ye Queen & so joyne wth ye King, or else with ye army to stay, & only give order for some regiments to wait upon her

William Barriffe, Lieutenant-Colonel of John Hampden's infantry regiment in the Earl of Essex's Parliament Army. Barriffe was wounded while serving with Hampden's regiment at the siege of Reading (15–26 April 1643).

Ferdinando, Lord Fairfax. Commander of the Parliament army in the North.

Queen Henrietta Maria. Self-styled 'She-Majesty Generallissima' of the small army that escorted her, and the arms shipment she had bought in Holland, from York to Oxford. The Royalist field word at Newbury 'Queen Mary' was probably a reference to her.

Sir William Waller. Nicknamed 'William the Conqueror' after a series of minor victories, Waller was decisively defeated at Roundway Down on 13 July 1643.

majesty. If he march'd up, his army would give a gallant addition to ye King's, but yn he left ye country in my Ld Fairfax his power, & it might be he should have him march in ye rear of him.' Newcastle held a council of war with his leading officers and resolved on 'sending some forces only with ye Queen, & try ye mastery wth my Ld Fairfax'. Newcastle sent two convoys south, the first under Colonel Thomas Pinchbeck with 1,000 men and 136 barrels of gunpowder, arrived at Oxford on 16 May. The second, accompanied by the Queen herself, left York on 4 June. The Queen's convoy reached Newark on 16 June, stayed there until the 21 June and arrived at Oxford on 14 July.

Newcastle's opponents were the Parliament commander in the North, Ferdinando, Lord Fairfax, and his son Sir Thomas Fairfax. The Fairfaxes had raised an army from Parliament supporters in the cloth manufacturing towns of the West Riding of Yorkshire, and Sir Thomas soon gained a reputation as a determined officer in a series of small actions in defence of barricaded towns and for attacks on Royalist quarters. Newcastle marched against the Fairfaxes' headquarters at Bradford and crushed their army at Adwalton Moor on 30 June 1643. Sir Thomas Fairfax retired on Bradford and defended it briefly, probably as a rearguard action to cover his father's retreat, but the town was untenable and he broke out with his cavalry. Caught up in a running fight, Sir Thomas only had two officers and three troopers left with him when he finally joined his father at Leeds. Sir Thomas's wife, Anne, who had left Bradford with him riding behind one of his officers, was captured in the pursuit. The Fairfaxes abandoned Leeds and retreated to Hull. Ever the gentleman, Newcastle treated Lady Anne Fairfax 'with all civility and respect' and provided a cavalry escort and his own coach to return her to her husband in Hull. The Parliament's Northern army had been destroyed and there was nothing to prevent Newcastle marching south if he chose to do so.

The War in the West

In the West Sir Ralph Hopton had raised a Royalist army formed of volunteers from the Cornish Trained Bands and the County *posse comitatus*. These Cornish militia troops had beaten Parliament forces out of Cornwall but they would not fight outside their county boundaries, forcing Hopton to raise five volunteer infantry regiments. The colonels of these regiments, Sir Bevil Grenvile, Sir Nicholas Slanning, John Trevannion, John Arundel and Lord Mohun, were all men of local influence. After the Royalist victory at Stratton (16 May 1643), Hopton's Cornish army was reinforced by infantry and cavalry from Oxford under the Marquis of Hertford and Prince Maurice, thereby creating a powerful Royalist field army in the West; a 'pretty marching army' as one Royalist officer described it. Hertford's infantry were mostly 'new-levied', and Hopton's Cornish infantry regiments formed the core of this new army. The Cornish regiments were amongst the best infantry to fight on either side during the Civil War. They were characterised by their fierce fighting spirit and a sense of independence that left them with little respect for any but their own officers.

Parliament commanders in the West had mixed fortunes in their campaigns against Sir Ralph Hopton's Royalists. Henry Grey, Earl of Stamford, saw his luck, and that of his Sergeant-Major General, James Chudleigh, run out at the battle of Stratton (16 May 1643) where James

Chudleigh was captured and changed sides. Hopton's next opponent, Sir William Waller, had earned the nickname 'William the Conqueror' in London for his series of successes in the winter of 1642/43. Waller was appointed commander of the army of the Parliamentary Western Association on 11 February 1643, and on 24 March he made a night-march to surprise Lord Herbert's newly raised Welsh army at Highnam, near Gloucester. Lord Herbert's inexperienced soldiers surrendered on terms and Clarendon commented, 'This was end of that mushrump [mushroom] army, which grew up and perished so soon that the loss it was scarce apprehended at Oxford'. Waller was defeated by Prince Maurice at Ripple Field (13 April 1643) and fought an indecisive battle against Hopton and Prince Maurice at Lansdowne (5 July 1643). Hopton was seriously wounded the next morning by an explosion when 'viewing the prisoners taken, some of which were carried upon a cart whereon was our ammunition, and (as I heard) had matches to light their tobacco', and his army fell back on Devizes with Waller's army in pursuit. The Royalist relief force of cavalry from Oxford under Henry, Lord Wilmot, Sir John Byron and Prince Maurice decisively defeated Waller at Roundway Down (13 July 1643) and shattered his army. The Royalists followed up this success by concentrating the Royalist Western army and a marching army of veteran troops from Oxford under Prince Rupert to besiege and storm the city of Bristol (26 July 1643).

Colonel John Hampden, Member of Parliament and a leader of the opposition to King Charles before the Civil War. Hampden was mortally wounded at a skirmish at Chalgrove Field on 18 June 1643.

Prince Rupert's Marching Army at the Siege of Bristol, July 1643

The main besieging force was a marching army drawn out of the King's Oxford army and commanded by Prince Rupert. This consisted of 'fourteen regiments of ffoot (but all very weake)' formed in to three Tertias or brigades of infantry, two 'wings' of cavalry, nine companies of dragoons and a small artillery train. Mostly veteran soldiers.

William Villiers, 2nd Viscount Grandison's Tertia
The Lord General's (Earl of Forth) Regiment under Lieutenant-Colonel Herbert Lunsford.
Colonel, Earl Rivers' Regiment under Lieutenant-Colonel John Boys.
Colonel Richard, Viscount Molyneux's Regiment under its Colonel.
Colonel Sir Gilbert Gerard's Regiment under its Colonel.
Colonel Sir Ralfe Dutton's Regiment under its Colonel.
Colonel John Owen's Regiment under its Colonel.

Colonel Henry Wentworth's Tertia
Colonel Sir Jacob Astley's Regiment under Sergeant-Major Toby Bowes.
Colonel Sir Edward Fitton's Regiment under its Colonel.
Colonel Richard Bolles' Regiment under its Colonel.
Colonel Richard Herbert's Regiment under Sergeant-Major Edward Williams.

Colonel John Belasyse's Tertia
Colonel John Belasyse's Regiment probably under Colonel Sir Theophilus Gilby.
Colonel Sir Edward Stradling's Regiment under his son Lieutenant-Colonel John Stradling.
Colonel Henry Lunsford's Regiment.
Colonel Sir Charles Lloyd's Regiment under Lieutenant-Colonel Edward Tirwhitt.

Cavalry Wings
The right wing commanded by Sir Arthur Aston, Sergeant-Major General of the Horse and the left wing by Colonel Charles Gerard. There is no complete list of the Royalist cavalry but it is known to have included:

Prince Rupert's troop of lifeguards under Sir Richard Crane.
The Queen's Lifeguard troop.
Colonel Lord Andover's Regiment.
Colonel Sir Arthur Aston's Regiment.
Colonel Samuel Sandy's Regiment.
Colonel William Eure's Regiment.

Dragoons
Colonel Henry Washington's Regiment.
Colonel Sir Robert Howard's Regiment.

Artillery
Two Demi-cannon.
Two Culverins.
Two quarter cannon (12-pdrs).
Two six-pounders.

Although successful, the storm of Bristol cost the Royalist armies dearly. Of Hopton's Cornish infantry 'there were slain, upon the several assaults, of common men (but such as were tried and incomparable foot) about five hundred, and abundance of excellent officers, whereof many were of prime command and quality' and they were never as effective again.

NEW STRATEGIES FOR A NEW YEAR

Essex had started his second campaign with a bold and well-planned move, marching against the Royalist garrison at Reading before the campaigning season had begun. His intention was probably to weaken the Royalist marching army by destroying a major contingent. However, the approach of relief forces weakened his position and Essex allowed the Royalist garrison to surrender on terms and rejoin the Royalist army at Oxford, although without the valuable gunpowder in the magazine. Whatever Essex's original intentions were for this campaign, the outbreak of typhus in his army prevented him from carrying them out. His weakened army was ineffective for several months following the outbreak.

The Royalist strategy for 1643 is harder to assess, but it certainly included the intention to increase the strength and effectiveness of their main field army. Strength was to be increased in terms of the concentration of troops to reinforce the main Royalist army based in Oxford, and effectiveness would be improved by securing sources of supply for munitions, especially gunpowder. Another key objective was to maintain pressure on the Parliamentary base, London, by bringing propaganda pressure to bear on the city. During February 1643 Royalist propaganda included threats that London's trade would be interrupted and the citizens starved into submission unless they influenced the Parliament to negotiate a peace. The successful campaigns of Sir Ralph Hopton in the West Country and the Earl of Newcastle in the North increased Londoners' concerns that the Royalist armies might converge on their city. In practical terms this was unlikely, as the local objectives of regional commanders and those of their soldiers made the Northern and

ARMA PACIS FVLCRA

Western armies reluctant to march too far from their bases. However, this was not evident from the perspective of London citizens hearing news of Parliament defeats, and it served to raise genuine concern in London and increase popular support for peace initiatives.

On a more basic level Prince Rupert introduced some of the more unpleasant aspects of the wars in Germany, including blackmail and unrestrained plundering, to English cities, towns and countryside.

CHRONOLOGY

1642

23 April King Charles and his army are denied entry to Kingston upon Hull.

22 August King Charles raises his standard at Nottingham.

23 October Battle of Edgehill. The first major battle of the Civil War proves indecisive.

12 November Battle of Turnham Green. The Royalist army's advance on London is turned back by the Earl of Essex's Parliament army supported by the London Trained Bands.

9 December The Royalist army go into winter quarters around Oxford.

1643

19 January Battle of Braddock Down. The Royalist Sir Ralph Hopton defeats Colonel William Ruthin's Parliament army and gains control of Cornwall.

19 March Battle of Hopton Heath. The Parliament commanders Sir William Brereton and Sir John Gell combine forces in an attempt to take Stafford but are beaten off by a Royalist army under Spencer Compton, Earl of Northampton.

30 March Battle of Seacroft Moor. The Royalist George, Lord Goring defeats Sir Thomas Fairfax.

13 April Battle of Ripple Field. The Royalist Prince Maurice defeats Sir William Waller.

15–27 April Siege of Reading. Following the real or pretended incapacity of the Royalist governor, Sir Arthur Aston, his deputy, Colonel Richard Feilding, surrenders Reading to the Earl of Essex.

25 April Battle of Sourton Down. The Royalist Sir Ralph Hopton is defeated by Major-General James Chudleigh.

13 May Colonel Oliver Cromwell wins his first victory in a cavalry skirmish at Grantham over the Royalist Charles Cavendish.

16 May Battle of Stratton. The Royalist Sir Ralph Hopton's Cornish army shatters the Earl of Stamford's Parliament army in the west.

18 June The Royalist cavalry commander, Prince Rupert, mounts an unsuccessful raid in an attempt to capture a Parliament bullion convoy. Pursuing Parliament cavalry catch up with him but are defeated at Chalgrove Field, where the prominent Parliament leader John Hampden is mortally wounded.

30 June Battle of Adwalton Moor. The Northern Royalist army under the Earl of Newcastle defeats the Parliament army commanded by Ferdinando, Lord Fairfax, and his son, Sir Thomas Fairfax.

5 July Battle of Lansdowne. Sir William Waller's Western Parliament army defeats the Royalist Cornish army of Sir Ralph Hopton.

13 July Battle of Roundway Down. Sir Ralph Hopton is besieged in Devizes. The Royalist relief force from Oxford, commanded by Sir Henry Wilmot, defeats Sir William Waller's Western Parliament army.

24–26 July Siege of Bristol. The Parliament Governor, Colonel Nathaniel Fiennes, surrenders after the Royalists breach his defensive lines.

10 August The Royalist army commences the siege of the city of Gloucester.

THE ART OF WAR IN ENGLAND 1600–50

Campaign Strategy

The objectives for a campaign could be set by a combination of political and military figures operating as a controlling group, for example the King's Council of War or a Parliamentary Committee. However, it was army commanders, not politicians, who determined the means by which these objectives were to be achieved. An army commander's campaign plans were, of course, impacted by his personal experience: by the generals he had served under, the armies he had fought with or against and the terrain over which he had fought. By 1643, there were two contrasting strategic styles in use in northern Europe. The first had been devised by the Dutch commander Prince Maurice of Nassau during the Dutch Revolt against Spanish rule (1567–1648) and the second had evolved during the Thirty Years War in Germany (1618–48).

The Dutch army fought its campaigns in a relatively small geographic area over a countryside where years of warfare had left even minor towns fortified. As a result, the main campaign strategy was to apply pressure by besieging and (hopefully) taking key strategic points. A significant success could have a domino effect because it impacted on the willingness of other local garrisons (which included the town's citizens who had their families and homes to consider) to resist and could lead to the capture of a whole province. The response was to seek to break the siege with a relieving army or, since neither the Dutch nor the Spanish had enough soldiers to form two effective field armies at the same time, to try to draw the opposing army away by besieging an important town or city garrisoned by the other side. The underlying requirement for this strategy was that both sides had to be able to field an effective field army because the basic threat of a relieving army was that it had to be able to fight and defeat the besiegers in battle. The Dutch leader, Prince Maurice of Nassau, created a well-trained, veteran army capable of fighting the Spanish on equal terms, and he put a lot of effort into circulating propaganda on the effectiveness of its training and new battlefield deployment styles. The Dutch army really was effective and it decisively defeated the Spanish at Nieuport (30 June 1600). However, Prince Maurice was reluctant to risk battle because his Spanish

Battlefield formations. By 1643 both Royalist and Parliament armies used a battlefield formation comprising two or three lines of infantry battalions, with the third line being used as a reserve to exploit a victory or cover a retreat. The first two lines were deployed so that battalions in the second line covered the spaces between battalions in the first line. The practical way to achieve this was for all the battalions in the first two lines to initially draw up in one continuous line. Then alternate battalions move forward, creating the correct spacing. However, this battle formation required open ground and enough space to deploy at the optimum distances. The enclosed terrain over much of the field at Newbury prevented it being used successfully.

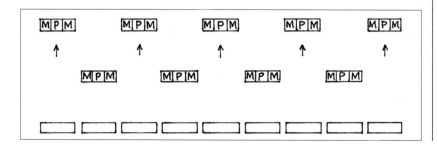

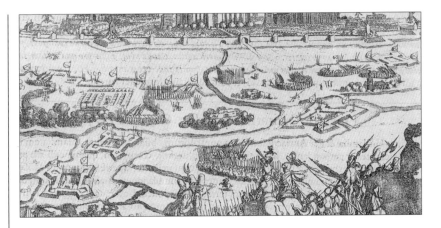

An example of defensive and offensive earthworks. This was the model used by both sides during the Civil War, although their ability to use it was restricted by time and the availability of an engineer to supervise the works.

opponents could replace their field army much quicker than he could, and the consequence of one battlefield defeat could have been the end of the Dutch Revolt. Maurice's successor, Prince Henry, was more aggressive but overall the Dutch strategic style remained cautious and focused on siege warfare.

The Thirty Years War in Germany was fought over far greater distances and over a countryside that was not as heavily fortified as the Low Countries. It was a terrain that offered opportunities for a commander, such as King Gustavus Adolphus of Sweden, whose strategic style was much more aggressive and who saw victory on the battlefield, rather than siege warfare, as the key to military success. It was also a strategy that offered the opportunity to win a war in one single overwhelming campaign rather than a long drawn out series of campaigns based on siege warfare. The impact of battlefield victory was not limited to the defeat of the opposing army. The knock-on effect of an outstanding military success, such as that enjoyed by Gustavus Adolphus at the battle of Breitenfeld (17 September 1631), was to persuade wavering opinion in the surrounding territory to join the victor's cause, thereby providing access to greatly expanded resources in terms of recruits, money and military supplies. Control of resources formed a key element of this strategy. Both sides would endeavour to dominate large areas of territory through the use or threat of force, sometimes by using fast-moving raiding parties composed of cavalry, dragoons, musketeers and light artillery.

The situation in England at the outbreak of the English Civil War in 1642 was closer to Germany than the Low Countries. English cities had not been fortified in the modern style and, although earthwork defences in the Dutch style could be built in a few months, there were few engineers in either the Royalist or the Parliament army who could set the design and supervise its construction. However, the military experience of most Englishmen had been in the English national regiments that served in the Dutch army so their strategic concepts followed the Dutch model. There were, nevertheless, some Englishmen, and more Scots, who had served in the Swedish or Protestant German armies during the Thirty Years War, and there were many more who had studied the campaigns in Germany and sought to emulate the remarkable successes of the great Gustavus Adolphus.

The Parliament commander, the Earl of Essex, had been a Colonel in the Dutch army, and both his military experience and his personal inclination followed the cautious strategies of the Dutch style of warfare. The leading Royalist campaign strategist was probably Prince Rupert. His practical experience was limited, but his impetuous nature and his studies of Gustavus Adolphus's campaigns led him to seek a quick end to the Civil War through a decisive Royalist victory on the battlefield.

Battlefield Deployment

The European military styles in use at the time of the English Civil War are described in Campaign No. 82, *Edgehill 1642*. These styles had evolved during the Dutch Revolt in the Low Countries, the Swedish campaigns in Russia (1611–17), Livonia [Latvia] (1621–26) and Poland (1626–29), and the Thirty Years War in Germany.

Four main battlefield styles were in use in Europe during the early 17th century, but by the 1640s the German style made famous in the Thirty Years War had become the most widely used. The Royalist general, Prince Rupert, had persuaded King Charles to use a deployment at the battle of Edgehill (22 October 1642) that was based upon the style developed by King Gustavus Adolphus of Sweden. However, it was a tactic that required veteran officers and men, and Prince Rupert did not have enough of either to use it successfully. The Swedish army, faced with the same problems, had abandoned this style in 1634. The Parliament's general at Edgehill, the Earl of Essex, had been trained in the Dutch style but he was well aware of other European developments and had deployed his men at Edgehill in a more modern formation based on the German style.

After Edgehill, Prince Rupert abandoned his attempt to resurrect the Swedish style, and by 1643 both Royalist and Parliament armies used variations of the German style. During 1643 Prince Rupert made extensive use of detachments of musketeers to strengthen his cavalry both on the battlefield and on raiding expeditions, a tactic pioneered by Gustavus Adolphus and which had now become part of the German style. The Earl of Essex continued to favour close co-operation of cavalry and infantry, a tactic that had served him so well at Edgehill. By August 1643 Essex had also adopted another tactic made famous by Gustavus Adolphus, attaching manoeuvrable light artillery pieces to his infantry brigades.

Siege Warfare

A new style of fortification, developed in Italy during wars in the 16th century, had been widely used by both sides in the Low Countries during the Dutch Revolt. In Italy these fortifications were built in stone, were hideously expensive and took years to complete. The advantage of this latest style was that it was designed to withstand the impact of modern artillery and to make the best defensive use of artillery firepower. In the Low Countries, the Dutch used the same style of military architecture but built their defences using earthworks rather than stone, since this had the advantage that the defences could be built quickly and relatively cheaply. However, the disadvantage was that after a few years of weathering in the rain the defences crumbled.

The Dutch army was trained to fight on the battlefield but its commanders, particularly its creator, Prince Maurice, were cautious strategists and preferred siege warfare to the risks of open combat. As a consequence, any English officers who had served in the Dutch army had first-hand experience of siege warfare in the Low Countries style.

OPPOSING COMMANDERS

THE ROYALIST COMMANDERS

King Charles I (1600–49) exercised command over all Royalist forces with the assistance of a council of war. Distance weakened his authority and he remained most influential in the South where he exercised direct control over his main army based around Oxford. The King had some understanding of military affairs because military theory formed part of the education of any prince in this period. He was also able to draw upon the advice of a number of competent and experienced officers. However, he had no practical experience of campaigning or warfare, and he had an unfortunate tendency to be swayed by the advice of the last man to whom he spoke. Some of his more influential courtiers understood even less about warfare than the King, and his decisions to follow their advice damaged the Royalist cause on occasion.

King Charles was present on the battlefield at Edgehill and Newbury and nominally commanded the Royalist army but relied upon his generals, particularly his nephew, Prince Rupert, to deploy and lead his army in battle. It was a sensible decision, since while his presence inspired Royalist officers and men, he did not have sufficient understanding or experience in warfare to take tactical decisions. However, the King's authority was final and the decision to besiege Gloucester rather than attempt to take it by storm was ultimately his.

Charles I, King of England, Scotland and Ireland, whose reign saw rebellion in all three kingdoms. (By permission of Dolphin Coins and Medals, Leighton Buzzard)

Patrick Ruthven, Earl of Forth, the Lord General (c.1573–1651) had replaced Robert Bertie, Earl of Lindsey, as commander of the Royalist army immediately before the battle of Edgehill. Ruthven was a Scottish professional soldier who had joined the Swedish army in 1606 and had risen to the rank of lieutenant-general by 1635. His extensive service in the Swedish army during its campaigns in Poland and the Thirty Years War in Germany made him a useful and experienced commander, although at nearly 70 years old he was probably past his best. Forth had made an unsuccessful attempt to relieve the Parliamentary siege of Reading in April 1643 and in August 1643 he was wounded at the siege of Gloucester.

ROYALIST HORSE

Prince Rupert (1619-82), who was King Charles I's nephew and one of the most influential of the King's commanders, was General of the Horse in 1643. Rupert's mother was the King's sister Elisabeth Stuart and his father was the German ruler Frederick V, the Elector Palatine, whose acceptance of the throne of Bohemia in 1618 had triggered the devastating Thirty Years War in Germany.

Rupert had practical experience before the English Civil War, having experienced both campaigning and siege warfare in the Dutch army. He

Prince Rupert, King Charles I's nephew and General of the Royalist Horse.

Sir John Byron. Commander of a brigade of Royalist cavalry at the battle of Newbury and the author of one of the two main Royalist accounts of the battle.

The cornet (flag) of Robert Dormer, Earl of Carnarvon, commander of a brigade of Royalist cavalry. He was 'run through the body with a sword' at Newbury 'of which he died within an hour'. The Latin motto *Reddite Caesari* is a Biblical quote (Matthew 22.21) that translates as 'Render unto Caesar'. (By permission of Partisan Press ECW Picture Library)

had also been captured at the battle of Lemgo in 1638 while serving as a cavalry colonel in his brother's mercenary army. While he was a prisoner, Rupert spent much of his time studying military theory and discussing the subject with Imperialist officers, who introduced him to the developing military theory of the Imperialist army. These circumstances provided Rupert with an unusually broad background in military theory. He was soon familiar with not only Dutch theories, but also the Swedish and Imperialist styles, and the developing composite German military style.

Rupert was a competent officer and a charismatic leader. His deployment at Edgehill had followed the Swedish style invented by King Gustavus Adolphus. However, this deployment had not proved successful, and Prince Rupert was left to spend the winter of 1642/43 reviewing alternative battle plans for use in 1643.

The Royalist cavalry were formed into five brigades at Newbury, one commanded by Prince Rupert and the others by Henry Wilmot (1613–58), Charles Gerard (1618–94), Sir John Byron (1599–1652) and Robert Dormer, Earl of Carnarvon (1610–43). Wilmot was second in command of the Royalist cavalry. He had led the left wing of cavalry at the battle of Edgehill with the rank of Commissary-General of the Horse, and he was promoted to Lieutenant-General of the Horse in April 1643. Wilmot, Gerard and Byron were all competent soldiers who had served in the wars in Europe. Carnarvon was a courtier with no professional military experience, although he had served as Lieutenant-General of the army in 1639 during the First Bishops War, and he had been General of Horse under the Marquis of Hertford in August 1642. He was described as being 'not only of a very keen courage in the exposing of his person but an excellent discerner and pursuer of advantage upon his enemy'. Carnarvon was mortally wounded at Newbury after he had 'routed a body of the enemy's horse, coming carelessly back by some of the scattered troopers, was by one of them who knew him, run through the body with a sword, of which he died within an hour'.

ROYALIST FOOT

Jacob Astley (1579–1652) was a professional soldier who had served in the Dutch army from the age of 18. He was a military tutor to Prince Rupert and a friend of Rupert's mother, Elisabeth, while Rupert's family were in exile in Holland. Astley returned to England to take up a position as governor of Plymouth in 1638 and was sergeant-major of the garrison of Newcastle during the First Bishops War. He joined the King at Nottingham in 1642 and was appointed Sergeant-Major General, 'a command he was very equal to, and had exercised before'. Astley took part in the siege of Gloucester, where the Royalist officer John Gwyn recorded that he was standing by Sir Jacob Astley when 'a bearded arrow stuck in the ground between his legs'. Gwyn also recorded that Astley 'plucked it out with both hands, and said "you rogues, you missed your aim"'.

The Royalist infantry were formed in four brigades or 'Tertias' at Newbury. The brigades were commanded by Sir Nicholas Byron, Sir William Vavasour, John Belasyse and Sir Gilbert Gerard. Both Byron and Vavasour had served in the wars in Europe but Gerard and Belasyse had no recorded military experience in Europe. All four brigade commanders were competent soldiers who had fought at the battle of

Edgehill; Byron and Belasyse as brigade commanders, Gerard as a colonel of his own regiment and Vavasour as lieutenant-colonel of the King's Lifeguard infantry regiment.

ROYALIST ARTILLERY
Henry, Lord Percy (1604–59) was the General of the Ordnance. He was a courtier, not a soldier, and most decisions were made by his able deputy Sir John Heydon.

THE PARLIAMENT COMMANDERS

Robert Devereux (1591–1646) **Earl of Essex**, had been Lord General and commander of the main Parliament army since its formation at the outbreak of the Civil War. He had seen some professional military service in the Palatinate under Sir Horace Vere during the opening stages of the Thirty Years War. Essex had been a colonel in the Dutch army in 1624 and was Vice Admiral in the expedition to Cadiz in 1625. He had been Lieutenant-General of Foot during the First Bishops War and had shown himself to be a commander who could identify opportunities and keep his nerve. Essex's strategy followed the cautious style of the Dutch army, with whom he had received his military training. Essex was well aware of the latest tactical styles and had set out a more modern battle deployment at Edgehill than his Royalist opponent, Prince Rupert. He was a competent battlefield commander, and as Clarendon ruefully commented on his deployment at Newbury, 'the earl of Essex had with excellent conduct drawn out his army in battalia … and ordered his men in all places to the best advantage'. The expedition to relieve the siege of Gloucester was Essex's greatest achievement during the Civil War.

Robert, Earl of Essex, Lord General of the Army of Parliament. Essex was a competent commander who had served in the Dutch army before the Civil War.

PARLIAMENT HORSE
Sir Philip Stapleton (1603–47) commanded the right wing of Parliament cavalry at the battle of Newbury. He was not a professional soldier. Stapleton had been commissioned Captain of the Earl of Essex's Lifeguard troop of cavalry in August 1642 and commanded the Earl of Essex's regiment of cavalry at the battle of Edgehill. He was appointed to command the regiment in early 1643 and was commissioned Lieutenant-General of Horse later that year.

John Middleton (1619–74) commanded the left wing of Parliament cavalry at the battle of Newbury. He was a Scots professional soldier who had served in the European wars and he had fought at the battle of Edgehill as a *reformadoe* or volunteer officer. Some accounts name him as the man who captured the Royal Standard from Sir Edmund Verney at that battle. Middleton was a capable officer who had been appointed colonel of a regiment of cavalry, formerly commanded by Lord Feilding, in November 1642.

PARLIAMENT FOOT
Philip Skippon was a professional soldier with a considerable military reputation gained through 24 years of service in the Low Countries,

Sir Philip Stapleton, commander of Essex's cavalry for the Newbury campaign. Stapleton led the Parliament right wing cavalry at Newbury.

Philip Skippon, Sergeant-Major General of Essex's army. Skippon was a professional soldier who had served in the Dutch army. He had been Sergeant-Major General of the London Trained Bands in 1642.

Denmark and Germany. He returned to England in 1638 and took up a position as Captain Leader (training officer) to the Society of the Artillery Garden in London in 1639. The society was a military guild that traditionally provided the officers of the London citizen militia, the London Trained Bands. In January 1642 Skippon was appointed Sergeant-Major General of the City of London with command over the London Trained Bands, and in that role he led his men to join Essex's army in the defence of London at Turnham Green on 13 November 1642.

During November Skippon was commissioned colonel of one of the new infantry regiments raised for the Earl of Warwick's new Parliament army and captain of one of the cavalry troops raised in the City of London. Essex, who knew Skippon from their days serving together under Sir Horace Vere in Germany and later in the Dutch army, had been impressed with the leadership Skippon had displayed at Turnham Green. Essex appointed Skippon to be Sergeant-Major General of his army in place of Sir John Merrick. Merrick was transferred to the post of General of the Ordnance. Skippon had the opportunity over the winter of 1642/43 to improve the level of training amongst Essex's infantry and establish his influence over them.

The Parliament infantry were formed into five brigades at Newbury. One was under Skippon's direct command and the other four were commanded by Harry Barclay, James Holborne, John, Lord Robartes and Randall Mainwaring. Barclay and Holborne were both Scottish professional soldiers who, like Skippon, had been commissioned colonels in the Earl of Warwick's army in November 1642. John, Lord Robartes had no known military experience before the Civil War. He raised an infantry regiment for the Parliament at the outbreak of the Civil War that fought with distinction at the battle of Edgehill. Randall Mainwaring was a London merchant prominent in the government of the city; he was a member of the Militia Committee formed in 1642 to manage the city's militia and was appointed deputy to the Lord Mayor in August 1642. He was also a leading member of the Society of the Artillery Garden and had been an officer in the London Trained Bands since 1628. In September 1642 Mainwaring was appointed colonel of one of the army regiments to be raised in London and had marched to Turnham Green as Sergeant-Major of the Red Regiment of the London Trained Bands. Mainwaring was appointed Sergeant-Major General of the City of London when the position became vacant on Skippon's appointment as Sergeant-Major General of Essex's army.

PARLIAMENT ARTILLERY

Sir John Merrick was a professional officer with experience in the European wars. He had been Sergeant-Major General in Essex's army in 1642 but there was no mention of him at Edgehill and he may not have been present at the battle. Essex appointed Merrick to the post of General of the Ordnance when he appointed Philip Skippon to Merrick's position as Essex's Sergeant-Major General. Merrick proved to be a useful artillery commander at Newbury, and a contemporary account recorded that 'the train of artillery that day was excellently ordered by the skill and care of Sir John Merrick, to the great advantage and safety of our army'.

GOVERNOR OF GLOUCESTER

Edward Massey (1617/18–1674/75) probably had some professional military experience with the Dutch army during the wars in the Low Countries. However, he is unlikely to have spent more than a couple of years with the Dutch, as he was still only around 20 years old when he took up a commission in England as a captain of pioneers in 1639 during the First Bishops War. Most young Englishmen who sought to become professional soldiers began their military careers in the English regiments serving in the Dutch army, which was a professional army that trained for open field warfare but saw most of its active service in siege warfare.

At the outbreak of the Civil War Massey joined the King at York, but he did not join the King's army. Instead he went to London and joined the army of Parliament as Lieutenant-Colonel in the Earl of Stamford's infantry regiment. The Royalist Earl of Clarendon wrote that Massey's decision was based on self-interest on the basis that in London 'there was more money, and fewer officers,' but this may not do justice to Massey. He was Presbyterian and, after seeing the formation of the King's army at first hand, his decision to fight for the Parliament may have been influenced by his personal conscience. Stamford's regiment was in garrison in Hereford during the campaign, which culminated in the battle of Edgehill. By the end of December 1642 the regiment had marched from Hereford to reinforce the garrison of Gloucester, and Massey became deputy governor of the city. He was appointed governor and held this position throughout the siege. He proved to be a resourceful and aggressive commander who took every opportunity to take the war to the besiegers, and he was able to maintain the citizens' resolve to defend their city.

OPPOSING ARMIES

By 1643 the theoretical strength of infantry and cavalry regiments bore little relation to their actual numbers in the field. It is, however, important to know the background of the individual units involved in a campaign, since veteran soldiers were better able to survive the hazards of campaign life and veteran regiments were more effective on the battlefield.

THE ROYALIST ARMY

The Royalists had concentrated two armies for the siege of Bristol in July 1643, one was drawn from their main army based at Oxford and the other was their regional army in the West. After the surrender of Bristol, Prince Maurice led the Royalist Western Army to campaign in Dorset and Devon, while Prince Rupert led the majority of the army he had drawn from Oxford to the siege of Gloucester. The Royalist army was weak in infantry and its commanders would probably have preferred to have combined their forces into one marching army. However, the Cornish soldiers, who were the best infantry in the Western army, had suffered severe casualties at the battle of Lansdowne (5 July 1644) and the assault on Bristol, losing several of their most influential local leaders. The Cornish soldiers now 'expressed a peremptory aversion to the joining and marching with the King's army'.

Clarendon commented that the Cornish were concerned that their homes were still threatened by the Parliament garrison at Plymouth and 'if they were compelled to march eastwards, to which they were not inclined, it was to be doubted they would moulder [desert] so fast away that there would be little addition of strength by it. Whereas if they marched westward, it would be no hard matter to gather up those who

Triple Unite, Oxford Mint 1643. King Charles set up a mint in Oxford in 1642. The coin shown here was worth 60 shillings, two days pay for a colonel. (By permission of Dolphin Coins and Medals, Leighton Buzzard)

were returned [had deserted with booty from Bristol] and to be strong enough in a very short time by new levies for any enterprise should be thought reasonable to be undertake.'

The army that Prince Rupert had led from Oxford had suffered casualties at the storm of Bristol, and it had been further reduced by the detachment of five infantry regiments to serve as a garrison for Bristol. Rupert's army had originally consisted of 14 regiments of infantry 'but all very weak' in three Tertias (brigades), two 'Wings of Horse' (each probably composed of a couple of brigades), nine companies of dragoons and a train of artillery. After the siege, Prince Rupert re-organised his infantry and led nine infantry regiments and a body of around 1,000 'commanded' musketeers (musketeers seconded from the regiments left in garrison at Bristol) to Gloucester together with the cavalry, dragoons and artillery that he had originally brought from Oxford. The Royalists needed more troops for the siege of Gloucester and obtained these from four sources: (1) additional regiments from the King's Oxford army; (2) detachments of infantry and cavalry from the garrison at Worcester; (3) the return of Prince Rupert's infantry regiments (now stronger following the inclusion of new levies) from the Bristol garrison; and (4) newly raised Welsh infantry under Sir William Vavasour.

ORDER OF BATTLE – ROYALIST ARMY AT NEWBURY

Infantry 6,000
Oxford regiments that had marched with Prince Rupert to Bristol

John Belasyse's Tertia
Lord General's (Earl of Forth's) Regiment
Colonel John Belasyse's Regiment
Colonel John Savage, Earl Rivers' Regiment
Colonel Sir Jacob Astley's Regiment
Colonel Richard Bolles' Regiment
Colonel Henry Lunsford's Regiment

Sir Gilbert Gerard's Tertia
Colonel Sir Gilbert Gerard's Regiment
Colonel Sir Richard Herbert's Regiment
Colonel Richard, Lord Molyneux's Regiment
Colonel Sir Ralfe Dutton's Regiment
Colonel John Owen's Regiment
Colonel Sir Edward Fitton's Regiment
Colonel Sir Charles Lloyd's Regiment
Colonel Sir Edward Stradling's Regiment

Regiments from Oxford sent to Gloucester during the siege
Sir Nicholas Byron's Tertia (incomplete list)
King's Lifeguard Regiment
Prince of Wales' Regiment
Colonel Charles Gerard
Colonel Sir Lewis Dyve
Colonel Thomas Blagge
Colonel William Eure

In 1643 a Royalist soldier's pay was 8p a day. Sixpence (Oxford Mint, 1643) (top) and a half-groat (Tower Mint, prewar) A groat was worth four pence, a half groat worth two pence (bottom). Most of a soldier's pay was taken up in deductions for his food, uniform and weapons. The obverse and reverse of both coins is shown. (By permission of Dolphin Coins and Medals, Leighton Buzzard)

Regiments from South Wales and from Worcestershire
Sir William Vavasour's Tertia (incomplete list)
Colonel Edward Somerset, Lord Herbert's Regiment
Colonel Sir William Vavasour's Regiment
Colonel Sir Samuel Sandy's Regiment

Commanded Musketeers from the Regiments at the siege of Bristol (1,000 musketeers)
Detachments commanded by Colonel Thomas, Lord Wentworth and Colonel George Lisle

Cavalry 8,000
Apart from two regiments (Sir John Byron's and Sir Thomas Aston's) that fought in Lord Byron's brigade in the centre, there is no record of which cavalry regiment served in each brigade. Regiments known to have served at Newbury are:

King's Lifeguard (two troops)
Prince Rupert's Lifeguard (one troop)
Prince Rupert's Regiment
Queen's Regiment
Prince Maurice's Regiment
Colonel Robert Dormer, Earl of Carnarvon's Regiment
Colonel Henry, Lord Wilmot's Regiment
Colonel Sir Charles Lucas' Regiment
Colonel Charles Howard, Lord Andover's Regiment
Colonel Sir Arthur Aston's Regiment
Colonel Samuel Sandy's Regiment
Colonel William Eure's Regiment
Colonel Thomas Morgan's Regiment
Colonel George Bridges, Lord Chandos
Colonel James Compton, Earl of Northampton's Regiment
Colonel George, Lord Digby's Regiment

Artillery
Two Demi-cannons
Two Culverins
Two 12-pdrs
Five 6-pdrs
One Saker
Two Mynions
Four 3-pdrs
Two Bases

THE ARMY OF PARLIAMENT

The Parliament had raised 20 regiments of infantry at the outbreak of the Civil War in 1642. One of these regiments, that under Colonel William Bamfield, does not appear to have become operational, but the other 19 were deployed during the Earl of Essex's first campaign against the King's army. After the indecisive battle of Edgehill, 15 regiments, some badly mauled at the battle, marched back to London with the Earl of Essex to defend the city. The other four were in garrisons. One was at Banbury, one at Hereford and two at Worcester. By August 1643 only five of his original 20 regiments were with Essex's marching army and only two others, Stamford's regiment in garrison at Gloucester and Aldrich's at Aylesbury, still survived. Although the number of Essex's original infantry regiments was declining, the infantry strength of his army had been increased in November 1642 by the addition of seven newly raised

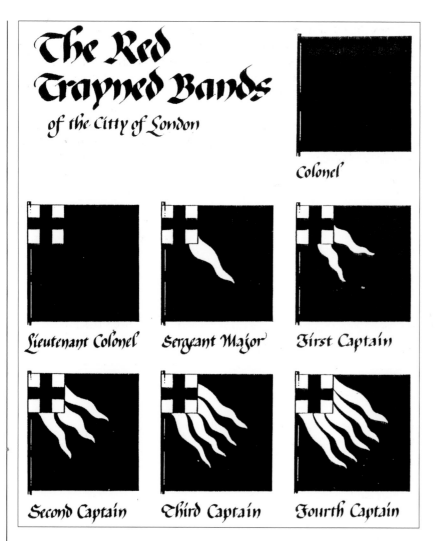

The Red Trayned Bands
of the Citty of London

Colonel

Lieutenant Colonel

Sergeant Major

First Captain

Second Captain

Third Captain

Fourth Captain

regiments. After Edgehill the Earl of Warwick had begun to raise a new army with recruits coming mostly from London and the county of Essex. These new regiments became part of the Earl of Essex's army on 22 November, and they continued recruiting during December 1642 and early 1643.

By July 1643 the infantry in Essex's marching army consisted of five of his original regiments, six of the regiments raised by the Earl of Warwick and one other, Francis Thompson's, whose origin is obscure. Essex would need recruits for existing regiments and the support of additional infantry regiments to stand a chance of relieving Gloucester. For this campaign his army was reinforced by two regiments raised by the County Committee of Kent (Sir William Brooke's and Sir William Springate's), one regiment from the garrison at London (Randall Mainwaring's) and a further five militia regiments from London. The London militia are described separately below. Essex had eight regiments of cavalry in his marching army and, for this campaign, was reinforced by three provincial regiments, a regiment of horse from the City of London (Edmund Harvey's) and some independent troops. In addition there were two companies of dragoons.

Essex faced a long march to Gloucester and back and had to consider whether to take only lighter artillery pieces in order to speed his march or take his heavier field artillery pieces as well. Heavier field artillery would slow down Essex's army but would also give him and his soldiers a better chance if they had to fight a pitched battle against the Royalists. There is no record of the size of Essex's artillery train for this campaign but it was known to be substantial, comprising heavy field-artillery pieces and a large number of lighter pieces. The Brigade of Militia regiments from the City of London was also well supplied with light artillery; 'eleven Pieces of Cannon, and three Drakes [light artillery pieces]' accompanied the militia when they marched out of London. Essex left his heaviest artillery pieces behind at Gloucester but evidently kept some with him as reference is made to two demi-culverins, and his use of a battery of field artillery (not light regimental pieces) sited on a commanding hill was a feature of the battle of Newbury.

ORDER OF BATTLE – PARLIAMENT ARMY AT NEWBURY

Infantry: 8,000

Sergeant-Major General Philip Skippon's Brigade
Sergeant-Major General Philip Skippon's Regiment
Colonel Sir William Brooke's Regiment
Colonel Sir Henry Bulstrode's Regiment

Colonel Lord Robartes' Brigade
Colonel Lord Robartes' Regiment
Colonel Sir William Constable's Regiment
Colonel Francis Martin's Regiment

Colonel Harry Barclay's Brigade
Colonel Harry Barclay's Regiment
Colonel John Holmstead's Regiment
Colonel Thomas Tyrrell's Regiment

Colonel James Holborne's Brigade
Colonel James Holborne's Regiment
Colonel Francis Thompson's Regiment
Colonel George Langham's Regiment

Sergeant-Major General Randall Mainwaring: The City Brigade
Red Regiment, London Trained Bands
Blue Regiment, London Trained Band
Red Auxiliaries, City of London
Blue Auxiliaries, City of London
Orange Auxiliaries, City of London
Colonel Randall Mainwaring's Regiment

Independent Regiments
The Lord General's Regiment
Sir William Springate's Regiment

Cavalry: 6,000

Sir Philip Stapleton's Brigade (Vanguard)
Earl of Essex's Lifeguard troop
Earl of Essex's Regiment
Colonel John Dalbier's Regiment
Colonel Sir James Ramsey
Colonel Arthur Goodwin's Regiment
Colonel Edmund Harvey's Regiment
Colonel Richard Norton's Regiment
Scout Master General Sir Samuel Luke (3 commanded troops)

Colonel John Middleton's Rear
Colonel John Middleton's Regiment
Colonel Lord Grey of Groby's Regiment
Colonel James Sheffield's Regiment
Colonel Sir John Meldrum's Regiment
Colonel, Earl of Denbigh's Regiment.
Colonel Hans Behre's Regiment

Dragoons: 150
Captain Jeremiah Abercrombie's Company
Captain Cornelius Shibborne's Company

Artillery
Essex left his heaviest artillery at Gloucester but had at least two demi-culverins at Newbury. He also had at least 20 light artillery pieces and drakes.

The London Trained Bands

The London militia, the London Trained Band regiments, were exceptional amongst the militia of the day because they took their military training seriously. The Trained Bands were the national militia, and they fulfilled a statutory obligation to provide themselves with arms and armour as infantry or cavalry and to attend formal training days to be taught how to use their weapons and how to march and fight in formation. For the most part, neither the Trained Bands nor their officers took much trouble over their training. The general view of their military ability at the outbreak of the Civil War was summarised by John Corbett in his *Historicall Relation of the Military Government of Gloucester* of 1645 with the comment 'The trained bands accounted the maine support of the ralme, and bulwarke against unexpected invasions, were effeminate in courage and uncapable of discipline, because the whole course of their life was alienated from warlike imployment.'

The London Trained Bands were different because of the efforts of the Society of the Artillery Garden, a voluntary association which originated under King Henry VIII and survives to this day as the Honourable Artillery Company. Membership of the society was drawn from the leading merchants of the City of London and its objective was to train them in the military practice of the day so that they could fulfil their roles as officers of the city's militia. The new, and very precise, Dutch infantry drill introduced by Prince Maurice of Nassau offered the opportunity to demonstrate expertise in the handling of arms and in precise manoeuvres on a parade ground. It was essentially an opportunity to show off, and it soon became fashionable amongst the leading citizens in London. One practical effect was that, in order to

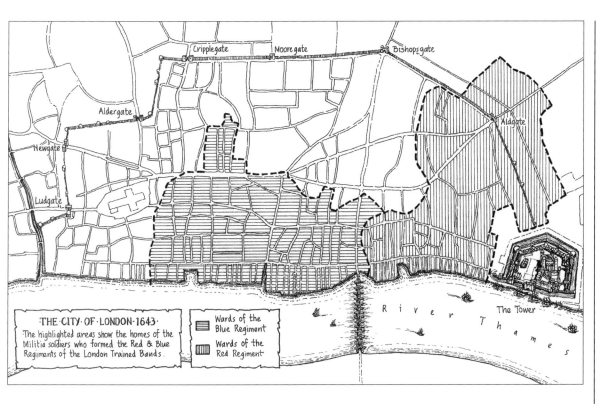

Cripplegate   Mooregate   Bishopsgate

Aldergate

Newgate

Ludgate

Aldgate

The Tower

River Thames

THE·CITY·OF·LONDON·1643·
The highlighted areas show the homes of the
Militia soldiers who formed the Red & Blue
Regiments of the London Trained Bands.

Wards of the
Blue Regiment

Wards of the
Red Regiment

excel in a fashionable sense, members of the Society of the Artillery Garden also had to be proficient in the basic military arts of the day and they hired leading professional officers to train them. Their training officer before the Civil War was the professional soldier Philip Skippon, who led the London Trained Bands at Turnham Green and then received an appointment as Sergeant-Major General in the Earl of Essex's army. Skippon's former role as training officer gave him a considerable advantage when the London militia soldiers joined Essex's army for this campaign because he was trusted by the soldiers and had personally trained most of their officers.

In February 1642 the London Trained Bands had been re-organised into six regiments totalling 8,000 men and these regiments had served alongside Essex's army to oppose the King's march on London at Turnham Green on 13 November 1642. During 1643 the city authorities had consolidated their control over the three suburbs of the city – the City of Westminster, Southwark and the Tower Hamlets. Each of the three had its own Trained Band regiment. In addition, six regiments of auxiliaries were recruited in the City of London and one in each of the suburbs, giving a total of nine Trained Band and nine auxiliary regiments. The City also raised cavalry. Six independent troops had been raised in 1642 and these were formed into a regiment under Colonel Edmund Harvey in 1643. A second regiment of eight troops was raised in 1643 under the command of Colonel Richard Turner. In all this represented a force of about 20,000 infantry and 1,000 cavalry.

Five regiments of infantry from the City of London Militia were selected for this campaign by drawing lots. Those selected were the Red Trained Bands, the Blue Trained Bands and the Red, Blue and Orange Auxiliaries. One regiment of City Horse marched with them.

The ensigns of the Blue Regiment of the London Trained Bands. From Levett's report. (Artwork by Dr. Les Prince. By permission of Partizan Press ECW Picture Library)

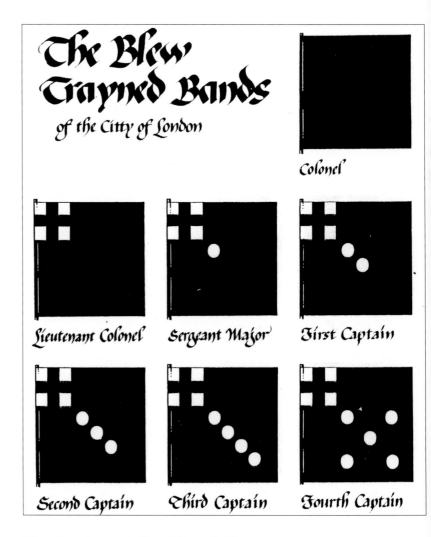

The ensigns of the Blue Regiment of the London Trained Bands. From Levett's report. (Artwork by Dr. Les Prince. By permission of Partizan Press ECW Picture Library)

The Garrison of the City of Gloucester

At the outbreak of the Civil War the only military forces in Gloucester were the City Trained Bands. In an increasingly uncertain world several cities raised auxiliary units during 1642 to support their trained bands and a company of volunteer infantry was raised in Gloucester in July 1642. Militia training varied according to the enthusiasm of the local lord lieutenant, or his deputy-lieutenants, and varied from one county to the next. A professional officer, Major George Davidson, was sent from London in February 1643 to improve the standards of the military training of the Trained Bands in Gloucester.

Small contingents from Parliament's army were left in Gloucester as marching armies passed through the region. The Earl of Essex's bridging train, under Lieutenant John Allerdine, arrived at Gloucester on 21 October 1642 and was left there when Essex's army retreated to London after the battle of Edgehill two days later. In early December 1642, Colonel Thomas Essex marched through Gloucester on his way to the West Country with two regiments, his own and Sir John Merrick's, which had been in garrison at Worcester. He left two companies of Merrick's regiment, under Captain John Lloyd and Captain Lower, to support the Trained Bands in holding Gloucester for the Parliament.

The Red Auxiliaries
of the City of London

Colonel

Lieutenant Colonel

Sergeant Major

First Captain

Second Captain

Third Captain

Fourth Captain

The Parliament provided reinforcements by the end of December by transferring the Earl of Stamford's regiment from Hereford to Gloucester under the command of its lieutenant-colonel, Edward Massey. The two companies of Colonel Merrick's regiment (Lloyd's and Lower's companies) were withdrawn to serve with Sir William Waller's army, but the garrison was strengthened by the addition of a regiment raised 'out of the town men for the major part both officers and soldiers'.

By August 1643 the governor, Edward Massey had a garrison of about 1,300 infantry and about 200 cavalry and dragoons. Massey's garrison consisted of:

The Earl of Stamford's Regiment (infantry)
The City Regiment (infantry)
The City Trained Bands (infantry)
The City Horse (1 troop of cavalry)
Colonel Arthur Forbes' Regiment (dragoons)

Uniforms, Weapons and Equipment
The equipment for infantry, cavalry and artillery is described in more detail in Osprey Elite 25 *Soldiers of the English Civil War (1) Infantry* and

Ensign of the London Trained Bands (c.1635).

Elite 27 *Soldiers of the English Civil War (2) Cavalry.* This section focuses purely on changes peculiar to 1643.

Both armies, Royalist and Parliament, made some effort to issue their infantry with new uniforms in 1643. In July 1643 Royalist infantry regiments in Oxford were issued with new suits of coats, 'some all in red, coates, breeches, & mounteers [montero caps]; & some all in blewe'. Most of the Parliament infantry in Essex's marching army were issued with new uniform coats, red or grey, at Bierton on 29 and 30 August during the campaign. Both sides were now able to obtain supplies of the latest pattern of lighter muskets for their marching armies, although the Royalist army did not have enough bandoleers and had to make up the shortage with leather bags worn on a waist belt to contain paper cartridges. These lighter muskets could be fired without the forked musket rest necessary for heavier models. Regional forces, the provincial regiments that were concentrated to support both armies during this campaign, were not as well-equipped. Many provincial soldiers did not have uniforms and had to make do with older patterns of arms and armour. Sir William Vavasour's newly raised Welsh soldiers would have been equipped with whatever could be scraped together from local armouries, some of it probably of Elizabethan origin.

The London Trained Bands were civilians with a statutory obligation to provide their own arms and equipment, and several different patterns were in use because they bought equipment over time and at their own expense. London Trained Band soldiers had no obligation to provide uniforms and wore their own civilian clothes on campaign. However there was a fashion amongst the musketeers to wear sleeveless buff coats over their civilian clothes. It was a practice that was significantly noticeable for the Royalist newsletter *Mercurius Aulicus* to refer to casualties at the battle of Newbury amongst 'the London Trained Bands and their Auxiliaries, many of whose Buff Coats our soldiers now wear'.

Unit Structure and Strength

The theoretical model for infantry and cavalry regiments is covered in detail in Campaign No. 82, *Edgehill 1642*. Essentially the theoretical model for an infantry regiment was a headquarters staff of eight officers and ten companies comprising either 1,000 or 1,200 soldiers (depending on the model used) and a further 110 officers. The theoretical model for a cavalry regiment was for a headquarters staff plus several troops. The optimum for a Parliament cavalry regiment was a headquarters staff of seven officers and six troops giving a strength of 360 troopers and a further 66 officers, 447 officers and men in all. The formal commission for Royalist cavalry colonels usually specified a strength of 500, probably meaning 500 troopers plus officers. At first sight this seems like a lot of officers compared to soldiers, but the term 'officer' was used in a different way in the 17th century to the definition used today. In the 1640s an officer was anyone who held an office or appointment and included commissioned officers, non-commissioned officers, musicians and specialists such as the regimental surgeon and his mates or the regimental provost. So, for example, a troop of Parliament cavalry comprised 60 troopers and 11 officers. Of the 11 officers only four, the troop commander, his lieutenant, his cornet (standard bearer) and commissary, were commissioned officers. The other troop officers were three corporals, two trumpeters, one saddler and one farrier.

Few colonels were ever able to recruit their regiments to meet the full strength of the theoretical model, and most faced even more difficulty in keeping their regiments up to strength under campaign conditions. At the outbreak of the Civil War men volunteered, or were encouraged in various ways to volunteer, to serve in both Parliament and Royalist armies and a charismatic colonel could recruit his regiment to something approaching full strength. By August 1643 the marching armies of both sides had suffered losses through direct casualties in battle, skirmish or siege warfare and lost even more through disease and desertion. In the spring of 1643 both armies had been decimated by typhus following the siege of Reading.

The net effect of this was that at the battle of Edgehill in 1642 regiments had sufficient strength to fight as separate regimental units, but by September 1643 many regiments on both sides were now so weak that they could not be deployed individually. For example, musters of Colonel James Holborne's regiment show that it had 660 men in February 1643, 473 in May and only 290 in August. In July 1643 Essex's officers complained in a formal representation that 'the number of the Foot are 3,000 marching men, and at least 3,000 sick, occasioned by the Want of Pay, ill Cloathing, and all other Miseries which attend an unpaid sickly Army'. Essex's officers went on to say that, 'The number of the Horse 2,500 (3,000 last muster) occasioned by the loss of Horses upon hard Duty and Service, and other Casualties incident to Horse in Service; Recruits of Horse, though often desired, not performed. Besides, by reason of a new Army [i.e. Sir William Waller's army], the officers find themselves neglected, the present regiments much lessened, listing themselves elsewhere for the new army expecting better Pay and Cloathing; and, upon their going hence, are entertained and protected.' This was a reference to the new Parliament army under the command of Sir William Waller, which attracted recruits from Essex's army as it was able to offer the incentive of immediate pay and supplies to soldiers whose pay was months in arrears and whose clothes were literally reduced to rags. The Royalist army was also affected by typhus and Royalist infantry regiments marching with Prince Rupert to the siege of Bristol were described as 'all very weak'. The London Trained Bands and auxiliary regiments serving in the Parliament army were stronger than regiments in the marching armies of either side because they were militia who had experienced no service outside the City of London before the campaign to relieve the siege of Gloucester.

Sergeant of the London Trained Bands (c.1635). One of the primary sources for this campaign was written by Henry Foster, a sergeant in the Red Regiment of the London Trained Bands.

MUSTER RETURNS OF THE EARL OF ESSEX'S ARMY

Infantry Regiments	June	July/August
Earl of Essex's (Lord General's) Regiment		726
Colonel Francis Martin's Regiment	275	250
Colonel Sir William Constable's Regiment	467	365
Colonel John, Lord Robartes Regiment	393	365
Colonel Thomas Tyrrell's Regiment		450
Sergeant-Major General Philip Skippon's Regiment	657	516
Colonel John Holmstead's Regiment	462	416
Colonel Harry Barclay's Regiment	636	496
Colonel James Holborne's Regiment	777	290
Colonel George Langham's Regiment	548	431
Colonel Sir Henry Bulstrode's Regiment	555	376

These returns are for 'common soldiers' only and do not include officers or NCOs.

Cavalry Regiments	June/July/August
Earl of Essex's (Lord General's) Regiment	391
Colonel John Middleton's Regiment	343
Colonel Sir James Ramsey's Regiment	incomplete return
Colonel John Dalbier's Regiment	219
Colonel Hans Behre's Regiment	154
Colonel John Meldrum's Regiment	361
Colonel Arthur Goodwin's Regiment	586
Colonel James Sheffield's Regiment	275

These returns are for troopers only and do not include officers or NCOs.

Army Strengths at the Battle of Newbury

Both armies left men behind in their march to Newbury, with the Parliament force marching hard in an effort to reach its home base while the Royalists made every effort to intercept them. Sergeant Henry Foster wrote that on the march back from Gloucester many Parliament soldiers were killed by pursuing Royalists because they had 'stayed behind drinking and neglecting to march with their colours'. Foster had little sympathy for men who failed in their duty, writing that they 'are not much to be pittied'. The Royalist officer John Gwyn wrote in his memoirs that, 'we made such haste in pursuit of Essex's army, that there was an account given of fifteen hundred foot quite tired and spent, not possible to come up to their colours before we engaged the enemy'. The Royalist Sir John Byron also commented on the impact of the Royalist army making so 'hasty and painful a march, that before he [Prince Rupert] reached Newbury there was about 2,000 horse and as many foot lost by the way'. John Gwyn's comment is probably more accurate as Sir John Byron's account is influenced by his dislike of Prince Rupert.

At the battle of Newbury the Royalist army probably totalled about 6,000 infantry, 8,000 cavalry and 20 artillery pieces. The only precise figure is for the artillery contingent, which according to surviving Royalist ordnance records consisted of two demi-cannons, two culverins, two 12-pdrs, five 6-pdrs, one saker, two (iron) mynions, four 3-pdrs and two (iron) bases. The Parliament army totalled around 8,000 infantry and 6,000 cavalry. However, it probably deployed fewer heavy artillery pieces because it had left its heavier pieces in Gloucester. The Parliament army did, though, have a larger number of light artillery, possibly as many as two pieces for each regiment.

A troop of cavalry and two companies of infantry supervise the destruction of the cross at Cheapside on 2 May 1643 by order of the Parliament. A rare contemporary illustration of Civil War soldiers.

Battle Formations and Tactics

At Edgehill there had been a marked difference between the tactical styles of the two armies, but by 1643 both sides were using variations of the German tactical style.

Apart from the battle formations themselves, it is also necessary to consider the depth in which infantry and cavalry units were drawn up. The Royalist army had copied the Swedish system at Edgehill, employing a unit depth of six men for infantry and three deep for cavalrymen. These unit depths were retained thereafter. At Edgehill the Parliament army had used the formations practised in England before the Civil War, with an infantry depth of eight men and a cavalry depth of six. Two contemporary accounts of Essex's campaign to relieve Gloucester show that by 1643 his infantry were deployed six deep. Sergeant Henry Foster, serving in the Red Regiment of the London Trained Bands, recorded that during the action against Royalist cavalry at Stowe in the Wold on 4 September the Earl of Essex formed his infantry into massive bodies,

Statuette of a Trained Band Pikeman from Cromwell House, Highgate (c.1638). (By permission of the Board of Trustees, Royal Armouries)

employing 'five or six regiments together, all in a body, about eight hundred or a thousand a-brest, sixe deep, we having roome enough, it being a brave champian country'. The second reference comes from the memoirs of the Royalist officer John Gwyn who recorded that on the battlefield of Newbury he saw 'upon the heath, lay a whole file of men, six deep, with their heads all struck off with one cannon shot of ours'. Parliament cavalry retained a unit depth of six men and employed defensive cavalry tactics. A Royalist account of the skirmish at Chalgrove Field on 18 June 1643 recorded that the Parliament cavalry were, still using defensive strategy tactics and 'gave us their first vollie of carbines and pistols at a distance, as ours were advancing: yea they had time for their second pistols, ere ours could charge them'. The memoirs of the Royalist cavalry officer Richard Atkyns show that that Parliament cavalry were still drawn up six deep at the battle of Roundway Down (13 July 1643), as he wrote that 'they [Sir William Waller's Parliament cavalry] being six deep, in close order and we [the Royalist cavalry] but three deep'.

There is no specific reference to Parliament cavalry unit depth during this campaign but contemporary accounts indicate that Essex's cavalry continued to make use of defensive tactics, relying on firepower (carbines and pistols) to break up attacking Royalist formations before making a counter-attack. For example the Oxford Royalist account referred to the Parliament cavalry at Aldbourne Chase firing a 'volley of Carabines given them [the Royalists] smartly at lesse than ten yards'. Essex also retained his preference for supporting his cavalry with formed bodies of infantry, and he demonstrated this tactic to good effect during the campaign.

THE ROAD TO NEWBURY

FROM BRISTOL TO GLOUCESTER

The Royalists had concentrated two armies for the siege of Bristol (24–26 July 1643). One was drawn from the King's army at Oxford under the command of Prince Rupert and the other was the newly formed Western army under the command of the Marquis of Hertford, Prince Maurice and Sir Ralph Hopton.

Ill feeling between the two elements of the Western army impacted Royalist strategy after the fall of Bristol. The King's options were, as Clarendon noted in his History, '… first, whether both armies should be united, and march in one upon the next design? And then, what that design should be?' The decision on whether or not to merge the two armies into a single Royalist field army had to be made first. The problem facing Royalist strategists was that the Cornish infantry, the core of the Western army, had felt slighted before the siege of Bristol by the imposition of senior officers appointed by the Marquis of Hertford and Prince Maurice over their own Cornish officers. The Cornish colonels were prepared to swallow their dissatisfaction for the good of the Royalist cause but their soldiers, whose humour was described as 'not very gentle and agreeable', were not. Furthermore, the Cornish soldiers also felt that their prowess was 'not enough recompensed or valued'.

The Cornish regiments had made their attack on the southern defences of Bristol with their usual elan but had been beaten back with heavy losses amongst both officers and men. Clarendon commented, 'there were slain, upon the several assaults, of common men (but such as were tried and incomparable foot) about five hundred, and abundance of excellent officers, whereof many were of prime command and quality'. It cannot have helped relations that the Cornish officers had argued against Prince Rupert's proposals to storm Bristol. They believed the defences were strong and that a formal siege would have been a better option. Many of the officers whose personal leadership influenced opinion amongst the Cornish infantry were now dead or wounded, and 'having lost those officers whom they loved and feared, and whose reverence restrained their natural distempers, they were much inclined to mutiny, and had expressed a peremptory aversion to the joining and marching with the King's army'. Opinion in the Royalist camp was that, if the Cornish were obliged to march eastwards as part of the main Royalist army 'to which they were not inclined, it was [not] to be doubted they would moulder [desert] so fast away that there would be little addition of strength by it'.

In these circumstances joining the Royalist Western and Oxford armies was not a viable option, and the decision was taken for the two armies to campaign separately. Other reasons could be given for this decision, for

Statuette of a Trained Band Musketeer from Cromwell House, Highgate (c.1638). The broad brim of this musketeer's hat has broken off. (By permission of the Board of Trustees, Royal Armouries)

39

An 18th century copy of an illustration from Henry Hexham's training manual, printed in London in 1637. Hexham's work was based on the practice of the Dutch army. Few English musketeers were equipped with helmets in 1643 and most used a lighter musket that could be fired without a musket-rest.

example the problem of providing horse fodder since the combined cavalry of both armies were too many 'to live on any country within a due distance of quartering'. However, this was not an argument against the combination of the infantry regiments, whose rations could be transported more easily. There was also the consideration that, 'if both armies had been kneaded into one, prince Morrice could have been but a private colonel. But there were enough besides … to keep them [the two armies] divided.'

Internal quarrels were always a factor in the Royalist high command, and after the taking of Bristol 'the sunshine of his [the King's] conquest was somewhat clouded, not only by the number and quality of the slain, but by the jealousies and misunderstandings of those who were alive'. The King resolved this by inviting the Marquis of Hertford to join the court at Oxford while Prince Maurice took command of the Western army, leading it away from Bristol to campaign in Devon. Prince Rupert was appointed governor of Bristol with Sir Ralph Hopton as his deputy. While Prince Rupert was absent on campaign with the King's Oxford army, Hopton was effectively governor of Bristol.

The big question, however, was what the next 'design should be' following the Royalist success at Bristol. One attractive objective was to take the city of Gloucester. An indication that the Royalists still sought to increase the strength of their field army – referred to as a 'marching army' by contemporaries – is provided by Clarendon: 'If Gloster were reduced, there would need no forces to be left in Wales, and all those soldiers might then be drawn to the marching army, and the contributions and other taxes assigned to the payment of it.'

Following the fall of Bristol there were considerable advantages in taking Gloucester, 'a city within little more than twenty miles of Bristol, of mighty importance to the King, if it could be done without great expense of time and loss of men'. The last part of this comment was the most revealing. The Royalists saw strategic advantages in taking Gloucester. 'It was the only garrison the rebels had between Bristol and Lancashire on the north part of England; and if it could be recovered, he [the King] would have the river Severn entirely within his command, whereby his garrisons of Worcester and Shrewsbury, and all those parts, might be supplied from Bristol.' However, the Royalists could not afford to become bogged down in a lengthy siege, as they would inevitably suffer further losses to their army while allowing their Parliament opponents to strengthen their force. Clarendon recorded that the factor that 'turned the scale' in this debate was the hope that the Parliament garrison commander, Colonel Edward Massey, was willing to persuade the citizens and garrison of Gloucester to surrender if the King 'came himself and summoned it'. There was certainly some communication between Edward Massey and a Royalist officer, William Legge, but Massey may only have intended to negotiate so as to give himself more time to prepare his defence.

On Wednesday 10 August 'the King ranged his whole army upon a fair hill, in clear view of the city, and within less then two miles of it, and then, being about two o'clock in the afternoon, he sent a trumpet with his summons to the town'. The trumpeter returned with two 'citizens from the town, with lean, pale, sharp, and bald visages, indeed faces so strange and unusual, and in such garb and posture, that at once made the most severe countenance merry, and the most cheerful heart sad; for it was impossible such ambassadors could bring less than a defiance.' The answer was uncompromising and stated they were 'resolved, by God's help, to keep this city'. Having delivered the city's answer the two representatives from Gloucester (councillor Toby Jordan, representing the city, and Sergeant-Major Pudsey, representing the garrison) 'on clap they their caps in the King's presence, with orange ribbons in them [orange ribbons being the symbol of the Parliament commander, the Earl of Essex]'.

The King's Summons to the city of Gloucester, 10 August 1643

'Out of our tender compassion to our city of Gloster, and that it may not receive prejudice by our army, which we cannot prevent if we be compelled to assault it, we are personally come before it to require the same; and are graciously pleased to let all inhabitants of, and all other persons within that city, as well soldiers as others, know, that if they shall immediately submit themselves, and deliver this city to us, we are contented freely and absolutely to pardon every one of them without exception . . . but if they shall neglect this proffer of grace and favour, and compel us by the power of our army to reduce that place (which by the grace of God, we doubt not we shall be easily and shortly be able to do) they must thank themselves for all the calamities and miseries must befall them.'

The city of Gloucester's response, 10 August 1643

'We, the inhabitants, magistrates, officers and soldiers, within this garrison of Gloster, unto his majesty's gracious message return this humble answer: that we do keep this city, according to our oaths and allegiance, to and for the use of his majesty and his royal posterity: and do accordingly conceive ourselves wholly bound to obey the commands of his majesty signified by both Houses of Parliament; and are resolved, by God's help, to keep this City accordingly.'

This was quite a terse response by the standards of the time, but it was clear enough. Gloucester would stand by its allegiance to the Parliament cause.

It was clear that the city would not surrender without a fight and, as Clarendon wrote, 'now was the time for new debates and new resolutions'. But some of the King's advisers considered that the form of the city's response was an affront to the King and 'in honour he could not do less than sit down before the town and force it'. In any case, ' . . . the confidence of the soldiers of the best experience moved his majesty, who, upon riding about the town and taking a near view of it, were clear of opinion that they should be able in less than ten days by approach (for all thought of storming was laid aside upon the loss of [at] Bristol) to win it. This produced a resolution in his majesty, not one man in the council of war dissenting.' It was with this sense of resolution that the Royalist army settled down to bring the city of Gloucester and its citizens to account for their defiance. The siege of Gloucester had begun.

21 Free your Cock.   22 Sword in Hand.

THE SIEGE OF GLOUCESTER

At first sight the Parliament governor of Bristol, Colonel Edward Massey, was in a weak position. He had only about 1,500 armed men in his garrison, although he was able to organise other citizens, men, women and children, to help with building and repairing the city's defences during the siege. He had insufficient artillery for his defences and only 40 barrels of gunpowder. The city's walls did not provide a complete defensive perimeter and the gaps had to be completed by earthworks. Massey did not have the time or sufficient experienced engineers to construct complete defences in the Dutch fashion but he did what he could, strengthening what remained of the medieval city walls by adding a yard and a half of earth behind them. He also filled in some of the gate towers with earth, cleaning out surviving ditches, adding earthwork bastions to some of the gates and building new earthwork defences to

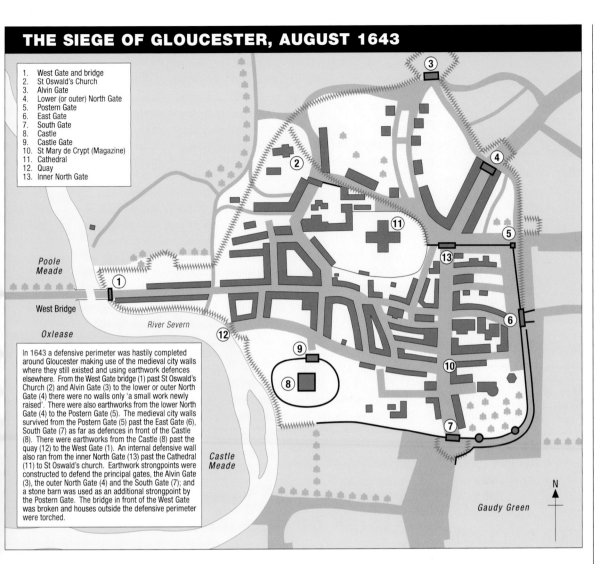

THE SIEGE OF GLOUCESTER, AUGUST 1643

1. West Gate and bridge
2. St Oswald's Church
3. Alvin Gate
4. Lower (or outer) North Gate
5. Postern Gate
6. East Gate
7. South Gate
8. Castle
9. Castle Gate
10. St Mary de Crypt (Magazine)
11. Cathedral
12. Quay
13. Inner North Gate

Poole Meade

West Bridge

Oxlease

River Severn

Castle Meade

Gaudy Green

N

In 1643 a defensive perimeter was hastily completed around Gloucester making use of the medieval city walls where they still existed and using earthwork defences elsewhere. From the West Gate bridge (1) past St Oswald's Church (2) and Alvin Gate (3) to the lower or outer North Gate (4) there were no walls only 'a small work newly raised'. There were also earthworks from the lower North Gate (4) to the Postern Gate (5). The medieval city walls survived from the Postern Gate (5) past the East Gate (6), South Gate (7) as far as defences in front of the Castle (8). There were earthworks from the Castle (8) past the quay (12) to the West Gate (1). An internal defensive wall also ran from the inner North Gate (13) past the Cathedral (11) to St Oswald's church. Earthwork strongpoints were constructed to defend the principal gates, the Alvin Gate (3), the outer North Gate (4) and the South Gate (7); and a stone barn was used as an additional strongpoint by the Postern Gate. The bridge in front of the West Gate was broken and houses outside the defensive perimeter were torched.

complete the perimeter. Once the Royalist army arrived outside Gloucester, Massey fired the suburbs outside the perimeter, a standard precaution as the dangers of buildings to the outer defences led them to be described by professional soldiers as 'the Cut-throats of Fortresses'.

Although modern defences served to strengthen a city, this was not enough in itself. The professional soldier Sir James Turner commented that 'some judicious persons, who have observ'd the practice of our Modern Wars in Europe these sixty years by-past; especially in the long German War, where many Forts were taken and re-taken, where many places only fortified in the ancient way, remain'd inexpugnable, notwithstanding obstinate Sieges form'd against them, having in them small Garrisons of Souldiers, assisted by stout and resolute Inhabitants; whereas other places of great importance, fortified with all the new inventions of Art, have either suddenly been taken by force, or soon brought to surrender on articles.'

Sir James Turner also commented that, 'the truth is, much of the safety of the place depends upon the Governor'. This was certainly true of Colonel Massey. He was an aggressive commander who was not only

Colonel William Villiers, Lord Grandison. Commander of a Royalist infantry Tertia (brigade) at the storming of Bristol, where he was mortally wounded.

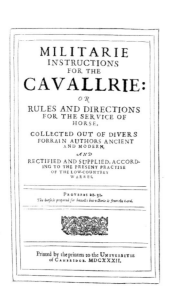

Frontispiece of John Cruso's cavalry training manual. First printed in 1632, Cruso's book was the most widely read cavalry manual prior to the Civil War. A new edition was printed in Cambridge in 1643.

able to maintain the morale of his garrison but also the will of the citizens to resist throughout the siege. Massey had the added advantage that King Charles had decided against the option of mounting an immediate assault on Gloucester. Bristol had fallen quickly to an assault but the casualties amongst the storming parties had been severe and King Charles was unwilling to repeat the experience.

However, Massey was not content simply to stand firm and defend the city. Instead he took the war to the besiegers by mounting frequent sallies against the Royalists, sometimes in considerable strength. The Parliament garrison certainly made life difficult for their Royalist opponents and earned their respect. Clarendon commented that the Parliament garrison 'behaved themselves with great Courage, and Resolution, and made many sharp and bold Sallies upon the King's Forces, and did more hurt commonly than they Receiv'd; and many Officers of Name, besides common Souldiers, were slain in the Trenches, and Approaches; The Governour leaving nothing unperformed that became a vigilant Commander. Sometimes, upon the Sallies, the Horse got between the Town and Them, so that many prisoners were taken, who were always drunk; and, after they are recover'd they confes'd that the Governour always gave the Party that made the Sally, as much Wine and strong Water as they desired to drink: so that it seems their mettle was not purely natural.'

For all the determination of governor, soldiers and citizens, they were heavily outnumbered and their resolute defence could only delay the Royalists. Gloucester was holding out longer than anyone would have expected, but the city would fall unless the Parliament sent its main field army to break the siege.

ESSEX'S EXPEDITION FOR THE RELIEF OF GLOUCESTER

Essex's expedition was widely reported in London because so many London citizens were directly involved, serving in the London Trained Bands and Auxiliaries and as volunteers or pressed men in Essex's main army. Families, friends and fellow citizens wanted news and accounts of the exploits of London soldiers, and London booksellers had good commercial reasons for meeting this demand. News was provided via entries in the weekly newsbooks circulating in London. Seven of these books were printed in London and one (*Mercurius Aulicus*) in the Royalist capital of Oxford. Several accounts were also written by men who had served on the campaign. Two of these eye-witness accounts are particularly detailed. One was written by several (unnamed) colonels of Essex's army and the other was written by Henry Foster, a sergeant in the Red Regiment of the London Trained Bands. These two accounts together with the newsbook reports make it possible to reconstruct a day by day account of Essex's march on Gloucester.

Each night the army was dispersed to the 'quarters' in which it would spend the night. The Lord General had the 'head quarter', usually in the largest town en route, and the rest of his army would be billeted in the same town and in the surrounding villages, farms or gentlemen's country

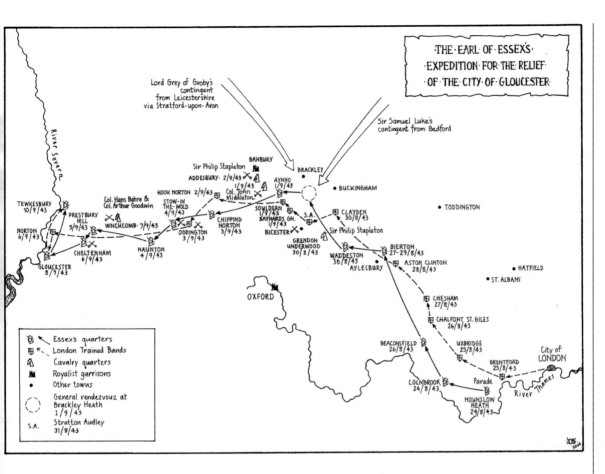

Lord Grey of Groby's
contingent
from Leicestershire
via Stratford-upon-Avon

Sir Samuel Luke's
contingent from Bedford

River Severn

BANBURY
Sir Philip Stapleton
ADDESBURY· 2/9/43
1/9/43
HOOK NORTON 2/9/43   Col. John
STOW-IN- Middleton
THE- WOLD
4/9/43

BRACKLEY
AYNHO
1/9/43
• BUCKINGHAM
• TODDINGTON

TEWKESBURY
10/9/43
Col. Hans Bahre &
Col. Arthur Goodwin
PRESTBURY
HILL
5/9/43   WINCHCOMB· 7/9/43
CHIPPING
NORTON
3/9/43
SOULDERN
1/9/43
BAYNARDS GN.
1/9/43
BICESTER•
S.A.
CLAYDEN
30/8/43
Sir Philip Stapleton

NORTON
6/9/43
ODDINGTON
3/9/43
GRENDON
UNDERWOOD
30/8/43
BIERTON
27-29/8/43

CHELTENHAM
6/9/43
NAUNTON
4/9/43
WADDESTON
30/8/43
AYLESBURY
ASTON CLINTON
28/8/43
• HATFIELD

GLOUCESTER
8/9/43
• ST. ALBANS

OXFORD
CHESHAM
27/8/43

CHALFONT ST. GILES
26/8/43

City of
LONDON

BEACONSFIELD
26/8/43
UXBRIDGE
25/8/43

BRENTFORD
23/8/43

COLNBROOK
24/8/43
Parade
River Thames

HOUNSLOW
HEATH
24/8/43

Legend:
- Essex's quarters
- London Trained Bands
- Cavalry quarters
- Royalist garrisons
- • Other towns
- General rendezvouz at
  Brackley Heath
  1/9/43
- S.A. Stratton Audley
  31/8/43

houses. A large army would use both the main road on its route and any parallel local roads. The regimental quartermasters (one per regiment for infantry and one per troop for cavalry) would go ahead to arrange quarters for the night and, where possible, provisions for the soldiers. The regiments in a large 'marching army' like Essex's would have to be dispersed at night if they were to find enough shelter. They would also have to be packed closely, with hundreds of men billeted in a single large barn. Even so there was often insufficient shelter for all of the soldiers and many had to spend increasingly cold nights in the open. The London Militia regiments found this particularly difficult as, although they had been well trained in the battlefield tactics of the day, they had no experience of life on campaign and 'were much straitened by want of lodging, and wanted other necessaries that they were formerly accustomed unto'.

The Earl of Clarendon recorded that the Royalist response to Essex's advance was to appoint Henry Wilmot 'with a good party of horse to wait about Banbury and to retire before the enemy, if he should advance, towards Gloster, and to give such impediments to their march as in such a country might be easy to do; prince Rupert himself staying with a body of horse upon the hills above Gloster.' As Essex's army came closer to Gloucester, Prince Rupert reinforced Wilmot with the rest of the Royalist cavalrymen.

Saturday 19 August
On 19 August a delegation of both Houses of Parliament attended a meeting of the Common Council of the City of London to support

The route of the Earl of Essex's march to relieve the siege of Gloucester, showing the parallel routes of the main army and the City Brigade (Londoners). Some of the outlying cavalry quarters can be identified and are shown here.

A PARLIAMENT SALLY DURING THE SIEGE OF GLOUCESTER

(pages 46–47)

The Royalist army followed up their successful storming of Bristol by marching on the city of Gloucester and summoning it to surrender. The Royalist commanders had hoped that the governor, garrison and citizens of Gloucester would be overawed by the fall of Bristol and give up without a fight. But they had misjudged the determination of the governor and the mood in the city. Representatives of the garrison and the citizens, Sergeant-Major Pudsey and councillor Toby Jordan, answered the King's summons to surrender by stating that they were 'resolved, by God's help, to keep this city', then 'on clap they their caps in the King's presence, with orange ribbons in them'; orange ribbons being the symbol of the Parliament commander, the Earl of Essex. King Charles had been horrified by the Royalist casualties at the storming of Bristol and would not risk further heavy losses by trying to take Gloucester the same way. This left no option but to commence a formal siege of the city, digging siegeworks and bringing forward heavy artillery to batter the walls. The city's governor, Edward Massey, mounted one of the most aggressive defences seen during the English Civil War and regularly sent out raiding parties from his garrison to attack the Royalist siegeworks. Here we see one of Massey's raiding parties attacking the Royalist soldiers digging trenches towards Gloucester's defences. Massey's Parliament soldiers are a detachment from his own regiment wearing the blue uniform coats issued to them the previous year. They never received a uniform issue of breeches or hats and wear those they had when they enlisted or have obtained since. They are equipped as musketeers (1) or as armoured halberdiers (2). The latter are drawn from the regiment's pikemen but equipped with halberds for close combat rather than the 16ft pikes they used in open battle. The Royalists are a digging party, their fully armed guards and an engineer officer in heavy siege armour. These soldiers are from one of the regiments sent from Oxford as reinforcements during the siege of Gloucester. The infantry from Oxford had been recently issued with new uniforms 'some all in red, coates, breeches, & mounteers [montero caps]; & some all in blewe'. This regiment received an issue of red uniforms. The guards are musketeers carrying a modern pattern lighter musket that can be fired without a musket rest but the Royalists were still experiencing supply problems and while two musketeers (3) have the usual bandoleer with powder containers, another (4) has been issued with a leather pouch containing paper cartridges, which he wears on his waist-belt. The digging party (5) are unarmed and use their entrenching tools to defend themselves. The engineer officer (6) is wearing heavy siege armour, intended to protect him from the defenders' musket fire as he supervises progress on the trenches. The background shows the wicker gabions used to create a parapet between the digging party and the city defences. The gabions were filled with earth from the trench. The trench itself would be dug at an angle to the city wall to prevent a lucky shot from one of the defenders' cannon ploughing down the trench and cutting down an entire digging party. At the head of the trench is a wooden barrier mounted on wheels (7) used as a moving barricade by the soldiers at the head of the digging party.
(Graham Turner)

Essex's request that the City send 'three or four of their Train's-band regiments, or Auxiliaries, to fight with the Enemy at that distance, rather than expect him at their own Walls, where they must be assured to see him as soon as Gloucester should be reduced'. The Common Council agreed to provide two regiments of Trained Bands and three of Auxiliaries for Essex's expedition. They also provided one regiment of militia cavalry (Colonel Edmund Harvey's City Horse) and the garrison regiment in London (Colonel Randall Mainwaring's Redcoats). The City Brigade was accompanied by 'eleven Pieces of Cannon, and three Drakes [light artillery pieces].'

Wednesday 23 August

The Red Regiment of the London Trained Bands was the first of the London contingent to be mobilised. It mustered at its company assembly points in London on 23 August and then marched to muster at the new artillery ground (the training ground of the Society of the Artillery Garden). Sergeant Foster recorded that, 'From thence that night wee marched to Brainford [Brentford], and came thither about one a clocke in the morning; from whence the next day many of our citizens, who seemed very forward and willing at the first to march with us, yet upon some pretences and faire excuses returned home againe, hiring others to go in their roome, others returned home againe the same night before they came to Brainford.' Brentford was a particularly evocative place for Londoners as it was the site of Prince Rupert's surprise attack on two London regiments, Lord Brooke's and Denzil Holles', on 11 November 1642 (see Campaign Series No. 82, *Edgehill 1642*, pp 86–91) as he opened the way for the King's unsuccessful march on London after the battle of Edgehill. Brooke's and Holles' regiments had been decimated at Brentford, and reports circulating in London claimed that the Royalists had murdered Parliament soldiers as they lay wounded on the battlefield and deliberately drowned other prisoners in the River Thames. Whatever the truth of these rumours, thinking about them must have made for a restless night for amateur soldiers marching out on their first campaign.

Thursday 24 August

While the London Trained Band regiments were marching out of the capital, or preparing to march, the Earl of Essex reviewed his army on Hounslow Heath. A reporter writing for the London weekly newsbook, *The Parliament Scout*, described seeing 'his Excellencie the Earle of Essex accompanied by divers Members of both Houses, and many Gentlemen with many officers, ride from Regiment to Regiment viewing them. It will be variously reported concerning his Excellencies power: Take this from our Scout, who made it his work to view them all over; he conceives their number amounts unto two thousand five hundred Horse, and some three thousand five hundred foote, a brave traine of Artillery was there likewise, and many Waggons, one following the other neare two miles in length.'

The *Parliament Scout*'s writer also commented that Essex's full strength was not present at the review because it was 'not a Muster but a Parrado', and 'many hundreds of the common men and divers officers were absent, besides these there are men that were prest to be added'. The point being that attendance at a muster had a direct relation to receipt of pay so there was a direct incentive to be there, clearly more of

Four Royalist cavalry cornets (flags) captured by the Earl of Essex when he 'beat up' the quarters of the Royalist cavalry regiments of Colonel Sir Nicholas Crispe and Colonel Richard Spencer at Cirencester on 18 September 1643. (Dr Williams Library)

an incentive than attending a 'parrado'. This 'parrado' did not include any of the London soldiers. The *Parliament Scout* commented 'there are also divers Regiments gone and to goe after his Excellencie from the City of London, all it is believed [i.e. all the London contingent], will amount to four or five thousand, which will make a brave Army.'

After the review, Essex 'removed his Quarter to Colebrook [Colnbrook]' where he was able to issue his men with a fortnight's pay as an encouragement before marching out on campaign, his soldiers were said to be much in arrears of their pay.

Friday 25 August

Sergeant Foster's account records that on 25 August his regiment 'advanced from Brainford to Uxbridge where our regiments were quartered there that night'. Uxbridge was probably the rendezvous appointed for the concentration of the brigade of London Trained Bands and Auxiliaries, and the London soldiers were now referred to as the City Brigade.

Saturday 26 August

The City Brigade 'advanced to a towne six miles beyond Uxbridge called Chaffin [Chalfont St. Giles], where wee were quartered that night'. At this town Sergeant Foster recorded an example of the frequent accidents with firearms that happened during this period when 'a souldier belonging to Lieutenant Colonell [William] Tompson was accidentally slaine by shoting off a musket by one of his fellow souldiers though at a great distance from him, yet shot him in the head whereof he died'. On the same day the Earl of Essex's army marched from Colnbrook to Beaconsfield.

Sunday 27 August

The Red Regiment of the London Trained Bands 'advanced from Chaffin [Chalfont St Giles] there to a village called Chessun [Chesham] This day the blew regiment of the trained bands and the three regiments of the auxiliary forces met us upon a great common three miles from Chessun, our whole regiment was quartered at one Mr Cheyney's house an esquire where we were well accomodated for beere, having great plenty, two or three hundred of us lay this night in one barn.'

Monday 28 August

The City Brigade marched from Chesham 'to a towne called Asson Clinton [Aston-Clinton], a little village three miles from Alesbury [Aylesbury], wee continued here one day and two nights'.

Tuesday 29 August

The City Brigade rested at Chesham. The Earl of Essex rested his army at Bierton near Aylesbury and issued new coats, shoes and snapsacks to most of his infantry. Essex reported to the Parliament that, 'Ye cause o ye laying still today was that the clothes and armes might be disposed of. The issue of clothing was made from St James church to officers, in some cases one officer collecting clothing for several regiments. The clothing consignment had included shirts but none had been issued, possibly because there were not enough for all of Essex's men and it was thought that to make an issue to just a few soldiers might cause dissension. Records show the issue of 3,336 coats, 4,260 pairs of shoes and 2,870 snapsacks.

Wednesday 30 August

Essex's army marched 'from Beerton [where the army was clothed]' to 'Waddesden [Waddesdon]'. The City Brigade marched from Chesham to a village called Clayden and from there 'this day the lord generall's army and our regiments of the trained band, together with the auxiliarie forces met at Alesbury; the great guns were fired at every fort about towne, as the lord general passed by.' Sergeant Foster recorded that 'our regiment was quartered at Sir Ralph Verney's house, a parliament man; his father the king's standart-bearer was slain at Edge hill.'

Thursday 31 August

Essex's cavalry commander, Sir Philip Stapleton, was quartered at Grendon Underwood on the evening of 30 August when he 'had advertisement that the enemy with four hundred horse was at Bicister [Bicester] three miles from him'. Early the next morning Stapleton sent out an advance party under Captain Robert Hammond which 'found part of them [the Royalist cavalry] drawn forth into the field to receive him, he thereupon sent a party to charge them, who beat them through the town [i.e. broke them and forced them to retire back through Bicester]'. The Parliament colonels' account recorded that 'This was the first time that we saw any enemy in this expedition.'

The City Brigade marched 'to a village called Stretton-Ardley [Stratton-Audley], this night all our brigade consisting of six regiments, viz. Colonel Manwaring's red regiment, two regiments of trained bands, and three of the auxiliary, were all quartered at this village, it is conceived wee were in all of this brigade about five thousand, here was little provision either for officers or souldiers'.

Friday 1 September

Essex's marching army joined with other Parliament contingents at Brackley Heath, the 'generall rendezvous' location that Essex had set for the concentration of his army. Here the 'the city regiments, and auxiliaries joyned with his Excellency his army; orders were given for severall quarters, the head quarter was at Aynoth [Aynho]'. The Royalist Earl of Clarendon recorded that recruits from Leicester and Bedford – 'the last recruits upon which he [Essex] depended' – also joined him at Brackley. The recruits probably comprised men from Thomas, Lord Grey of Groby's and Lord Denbigh's cavalry regiments and some cavalry troops from Bedford under Sir Samuel Luke.

Sergeant Foster recalled that the City Brigade was in good spirits when 'our brigade met my lord generall with his whole army, whereat

Five Royalist cornets (cavalry flags) and two bare standard poles captured by the Earl of Essex in the same engagement in which the Royalist cornets opposite were captured. (Dr Williams Library)

Front.

E.   C.

```
S. M M M M D P P P P P P P P D M M M M S
W M M M M   P P P P P P P P   M M M M  W
W M M M M   P P P P P P P P   M M M M  W
W M M M M   P P P P P P P P   M M M M  W
W M M M M   P P P P P P P P   M M M M  W
W M M M M   P P P P P P P P   M M M M  W
  M M M M   P P P P P P P P   M M M M
S. • • • • D P P P P P P P P D • • • • S
                  L.
            Reere.
```

Front.

```
S M M M M                        M M M M S
W                                        W
W                                        W
W              E.  C.                    W
S W M M M M D P P P P P P P P P.D M M M M S
  M M M M     P P P P P P P P     M M M M
  M M M M     P P P P P P P P     M M M M
  M M M M     P P P P P P P P     M M M M
  M M M M     P P P P P P P P     M M M M
  M M M M     P P P P P P P P     M M M M
  • • • •     P P P P P P P P     • • • •
  • • • • D P P P P P P P P P D • • • •
                  L.
            Reere.
```

Firing systems. Two of several systems where musketeers fired rank by rank and then retired to the rear of their file to re-load. Contemporary training manuals illustrated these formations using a single company, but in action several companies were combined.

was great shouting and triumph as he passed by to take a view of our regiments; the whole army being drawne up in their severall regiments, continued there about an houre and then we marched away: it was a goodly and glorious sight to see the whole army of horse and foot together; it is conceived by those that viewed our army well, that wee did consist of (to speak of the least) fifteen thousand horse and foot, some speak of many more.' Following the review, the City Brigade marched 'to a village called Souldern, foure miles from Banbury, where our six regiments that came from London were quartered; and my lord general and the rest of the army were quartered about a mile from us, at a market town called Ano on the Hill [Aynho].' Sergeant Foster recalled that, 'We were very much scanted of victualls in this place.'

The Parliament Colonel John Middleton, who was second in command of the cavalry, was on his way to his allocated quarters at

Deddington, 'and hearing there of two regiments of the enemie's horse, sent Captain Middleton with two companies of dragoons, and Captain Hale with a party of horse to approach the town, but the enemy retreated to a passage toward Oxford where the Lord Wilmot was with fifty troops more. Our scouts followed so far that they encountered with the other [Royalist] scouts, and fired at each other.' This was the first contact with the main body of the Royalist cavalry, which had been sent out under Henry Wilmot to slow down Essex's advance.

Saturday 2 September

That morning Colonel Middleton with his own and Sir James Ramsey's regiments of cavalry and two companies of dragoons covered Essex's army from attack by Wilmot's Royalist cavalry as the Parliament soldiers continued their march to Gloucester. Middleton's regiments then formed the rearguard of the army and fought off a Royalist attack. That night Essex's headquarters was at Adderbury. The City Brigade was quartered at 'Hooknorton [Hook Norton], twenty-five miles from Glocester'.

Sunday 3 September

After divine service Essex's army 'marched to Chipping-Norton, where presently after their quartering, the enemy appeared neare the towne; but soon retreated upon the first advance of Sir James Ramsey and Colonel Beere [Hans Behre] with his regiment of horse.'

The City Brigade marched 'to a little village called Addington [Oddington] about a mile from Stow the Old [Stowe on the Wold], the hithermost town in Glocester-shire, and about twenty miles for Glocester; where in our march this day, wee againe met with the lord generall's army, upon a great common about halfe a mile from Chippingnorton, at which place our five regiments departed his army and marched to the village aforesaid.' The 'blew regiment of the train's bands' which was in the van of the City Brigade took up quarters in Chipping Norton itself, and the 'auxiliary regiments were quartered in

George, Lord Digby was a Royalist cavalry colonel at Edgehill. Digby gave up command of his regiment to join the court. His letter describing the battle was published in Oxford shortly after the battle.

The Marching Postures   *Of the Harquebusiers.*

Arquebusiers from an 18th-century copy of illustrations from John Cruso's cavalry manual. By 1643 most cavalrymen were equipped with English tri-bar or European *zischagge* helmets.

the villages adjacent'. However, the red regiment 'was constrained to march halfe a mile further to get quarter, we were now in the van of the whole army, having not so much a troop of horse quartered neer us'. The Red Trained Bands 'were no sooner in our quarters, and set downe our armes, intending a little to refresh ourselves; but presently there was an alarme beat up [probably in response to the Royalist cavalry attack beaten off by Colonels Ramsey and Behre], and wee being the frontier regiment nearest the army were presently all drawn up into a body, and stood upon our guard all that night, we were in great distraction, having not any horse to send out as scouts, to give us any intelligence.' The Red Trained Bands had an unpleasant night as they 'stood in the open field all night, having neither bread nor water to refresh ourselves, having also marched the day before without any sustenance, neither durst we kindle any fire though it was a cold night'.

A message shot into the city of Gloucester from the Royalist Siege Lines, 3 September 1643

'These are to let you understand that your god Waller hath forsaken you, and hath retired himselfe to the Tower of London. Essex is beaten like a dog; yeelde to the Kings mercie in time, otherwise, if we enter perforce, no quarter, for such obstinate traiterly rogues. From a well wisher.'

The reply from the city of Gloucester

Waller's no god of ours, base rogues you lie,
Our God survives from all eternity;
Though essex beaten be, as you doe say,
Rome's yoke we are resolv'd nere to obey;
But for our cabages which ye have eaten
Be sure ere long ye shall be soundly beaten.
Quarter we ask you none; if we fall downe,
King Charles will lose true subjects with the towne.

Monday 4 September

Wilmot had not made much impact on the Parliament army so far but, after his unsuccessful attempt to beat up Essex's quarters at Chipping Norton, he must have received intelligence of where the City Brigade was quartered. Inexperienced soldiers without any cavalry support for scouts should have been easy to surprise, but Wilmot missed his opportunity. Instead of attacking at dawn when the Royalist cavalry might have 'spoiled our whole regiment, had they in the morning come down upon us while we were taking a little food to refresh ourselves', the Royalists left it too late. Hearing the 'enemy was within halfe a mile of the town' and concerned that their quarters were 'a little open village, the enemy might have come in upon us every way', the Red Trained Bands 'conceiving it not safe to abide in the town, drew up our regiment presently into a body and marched into a broad open field to the top of the hill'. The Trained Band soldiers found themselves surrounded by three large formations of Royalist cavalry but held their ground until the auxiliary regiments and then Essex's main army came up in support.

Prince Rupert had joined Wilmot on 4 September with most of the Royalist cavalry from the King's army at the siege of Gloucester; and it is possible that Wilmot was waiting for these reinforcements

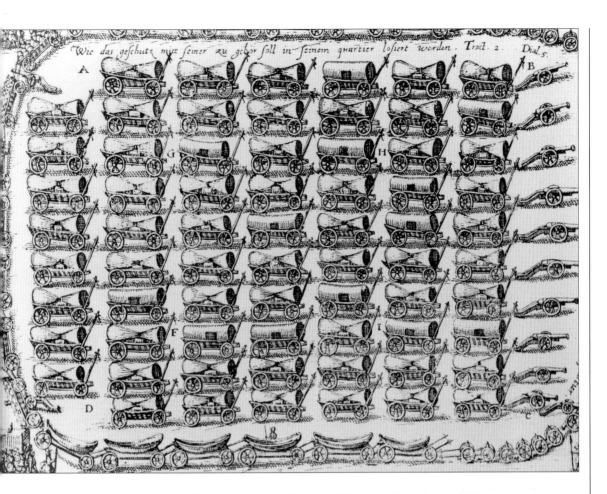

Wie das geschutz mit seiner zu gehor soll in seinem quartier losiert werden. Tract. 2. Dial. 5.

An army on the march required a large support train to carry its provisions, ammunition, spare weapons and artillery supplies.

before he committed any of his men. By doing so Wilmot would ensure his cavalrymen were fresh and ready for battle. The combined Royalist cavalry continued to face Essex's army as it moved forward in battle formation but they were unable to prevent its advance. The Royalists had neither infantry nor artillery to support their cavalry, and Essex used his artillery to fire on the Royalists while his infantry advanced 'towards them five or six regiments together, all in a body, about eight hundred or a thousand abreast, sixe deep, we having roome enough, it being a brave champion [open] country'. This was exactly the type of open country where the King's military advisers had believed that the superiority of the Royalist cavalry would stop the Parliament army. By using his infantry, cavalry and artillery in co-operation Essex prevented the Royalists from gaining any advantage.

Tuesday 5 September

Essex's army reached Prestbury Hills within sight of Gloucester 'where he drew up his whole army in view of the city of Gloucester, and discharged 4 peeces of great ordinance to give them notice of his approach; soon after we discovered the enemie's quarters on fire, for upon our advance they deserted the siege.' The citizens of Gloucester marked the end of the siege on 5 September with an inscription upon the rebuilt South Gate of the city. The inscription read: 'A City assaulted by Man but saved by God' on one side, and 'Ever remember the Vth Sept. 1643' on the other.

The Earl of Essex left his 'boats upon carriages' in Gloucester when he retreated to London in October 1642. The bridging train and its commander, Lieutenant John Allerdine, were still there when the city was besieged.

Wednesday 6 September

Essex marched, unopposed, to Cheltenham. The Royalists beat up the quarters of Colonel John Dalbier's cavalry overnight but failed to surprise them and 'soon retired with little losse'.

Thursday 7 September

The Royalist cavalry 'beat up the quarters of Colonell [Arthur] Goodwin and Colonell Beere [Hans Behre] at Winscome'. The outlying Parliament guard under Sergeant-Major Samuel Boza fulfilled its function to buy time for the main body of cavalry to form up and lost a cavalry standard in the skirmish. Apart from this, the Parliament loss 'was not considerable' and the Royalist attack failed.

Essex's army stayed around Cheltenham that day. The City Brigade was quartered around 'a little village called Norton'. The Londoners were exhausted and when around 'seven of the clock there came a command for our regiments of the trained bands to march five miles back again [back towards Essex's main force] in the night, but it being a very darke night, and our men worn out and spent with their former marching, they refused to goe; but next morning, being Friday, September 8, we did.'

Friday 8 September

Sergeant Foster recorded that, 'The lord generall with the whole army marched into Gloucester this day,' adding that 'wee found very loving respect and entertainment in this citie, they being very joyful of our coming; wee abode here Fryday night and Saturday, and marched away on Sabbath day morning: the lord generall left in this citie three great pieces of ordnance, as also many score barrels of powder, with match and bullet proportionable, furnishing them to their hearts desire'.

Sunday 10 September

On Sunday Essex marched to Tewkesbury to place his army between Gloucester and the King's army while he and the city's governor, Colonel Massey, made arrangements to sweep up local supplies and re-provision Gloucester. In order to deceive the Royalists as to his next move Essex 'gave order for the making of a bridge over the river Severne neere Tewksbury, as if our intention had been to march with our army over there to Worcester', possibly using the pontoon bridge train that had been left in Gloucester the year before.

ESSEX'S FIGHTING RETREAT BACK TO LONDON (15–19 SEPTEMBER)

The Earl of Essex had achieved the first part of his objective when he relieved the siege of the city of Gloucester. That had not been easy but the hardest part remained, now he had to get his army back to its base in one piece. Essex had heavy field artillery with him and the London militia regiments serving in his army were unused to campaigning. He knew that both factors would slow down his march and he needed a head start on his Royalist opponents.

The Royalist account of Newbury admitted that Essex's next move had fooled his opponents completely, 'upon intelligence that the Earle was advanced as far as Teuxbury and Upton bridge (whereby it was made possible to us that he intended Warwicke way) the king removed his army of Evesham, from whence having beaten up a quarter of theirs we were quickly hurried by the newes that Essex had faced about, and had in the night, with great silence, secrecy and strange dilgence, almost gained Cirencester, and surprised two new raised regiments of ours there before we could get any certain notice of his motions'.

Edward Massey, Governor of the city of Gloucester. Massey was a professional soldier who had served in the Dutch army.

Friday 15 September

On the morning of 15 September, the Earl of Essex's army marched out of Tewkesbury to start its march back to its base around London. Essex marched to Cirencester on receipt of intelligence that a body of the enemies horse 'were then in Cirencester (which was reported to be Prince Maurice his forces) and had there laid in great store of provision for their army (our want of necessaries and victual still continuing, and miserably encreasing upon us)'. Essex made a forced march and reached Cirencester early on the morning of 16 September (variously reported as one o'clock or three o'clock in the morning). The Royalist force consisted of two newly raised regiments of Horse, Colonel Sir Nicholas Crispe's and Colonel Richard Spencer's. The Parliament soldiers mounted a professional attack on their inexperienced opponents, their 'forlorne hope entred the town whilst the rest surrounded it, killed the sentinell sleeping, marched up to the market place without opposition (the enemy supposing them Prince Maurice his forces, that night expected) till they entred the houses and surprized them in bed'. One of the Parliament soldiers recorded that, as distinguishing field signs for this action, 'we all had white handkerchiefs in our hats and the word "God" in our mouths for distinction'.

Saturday 16 September

Essex's men had captured between 200 and 300 prisoners at Cirencester as well as 11 cavalry standards, 400 horses and 30–40 cartloads of provisions. Some of the prisoners from Sir Nicholas Crispe's Regiment were from London, including 'one Mason, an upholsterer in Newgate Market' and 'one Captain Hacker' – Richard Hacket, formerly a captain in the Blue regiment of the London Trained Bands. It must have been an interesting meeting for Captain Hacket, as many of the soldiers in the Trained Band company he had commanded were amongst those who captured him.

The Parliament army made a short march of five miles that day, taking their prisoners with them tied 'two and two together with match'. The City Brigade was quartered that night at a 'village called Letton; the lord generall with his army quartered a mile further at a market-towne in Wiltshire called Cricklet [Cricklade].'

Sunday 17 September

Sergeant Foster recorded 'Sabbath day, September 17, we marched from Cricklet [Cricklade] to a market towne called Swindowne [Swindon], eight miles'. The Parliament Official account recorded that at Swindon the Parliament army 'had a sermon in the afternoon'.

On the same day a letter was written by Lord George Digby and was sent by the King to Prince Rupert. 'The King has received your Highness's letter written from Stamford, at five of the clock this evening, and commands me thereupon to let your Highness know, that since it appears by your intelligence that my Lord of Essex is not so far out of reach as was feared, he is desirous to make all haste towards him; his Majesty's army being all except stragglers, well up hither to Alvesscott.' Lord Digby added, 'I am commanded to add, that you should consider to allow the foot here as much rest as can well be without losing the opportunity.'

A Letter from Home

A letter from Susan Owen to her 'dear husband Master John Owen under Lieutenant Colonel [Francis] West in the Blue regiment [London Trained Bands]' dated 5 September 1643. The letter was intercepted by Royalist patrols and published by the Royalist weekly newsbook in its edition for 3–9 September.

> *'Most tender and dear heart, my kind affection remembered unto you. I am like never to see you more I fear, and if you ask the reason why, the reason is this, either I am afraid the Cavaliers will kill you or death will deprive you of me, being full of grief for you, which I fear will cost me my life. I do much grieve that you be so hard-hearted to me. Why could not you come home with Master Murphy on Saturday? Could not you venture as well as he? But you did it on purpose to show your hatred to me. There is none of our neighbours with you that has a wife but Master Fletcher and Master Norwood and yourself. Everybody can come but you. I have sent one to Oxford to get a pass for you to come home, but when you come you must use your wits. I am afraid if you do not come home, I shall much dishonour God more than you can honour him. Therefore if I do miscarry, you shall answer for it. Pity me for God's sake and come home. Will nothing prevail with you? My cousin Jane is now with me and prays for your speedy return. For God's sake come home. So with my prayer for you I rest your loving wife.'*
>
> *London, 5 September*
> *Susan Owen*

Monday 18 September

At one o'clock in the morning, the King sent another dispatch to Prince Rupert. The King 'approves of all of it [a dispatch from Prince Rupert] and will accordingly perform his part, only desires to have certain knowledge when Essex moved, or shall move from Cricklade, that if His

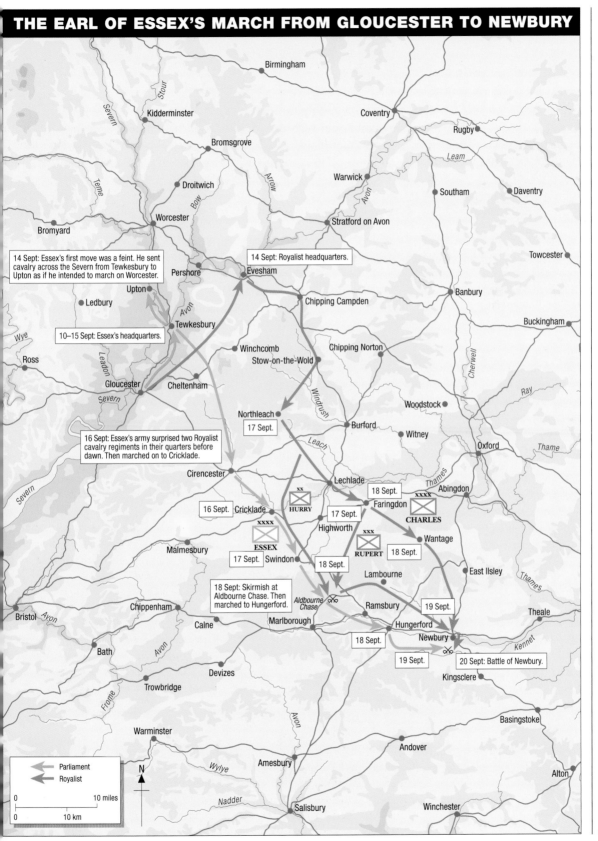

14 Sept: Essex's first move was a feint. He sent cavalry across the Severn from Tewkesbury to Upton as if he intended to march on Worcester.

14 Sept: Royalist headquarters.

10–15 Sept: Essex's headquarters.

16 Sept: Essex's army surprised two Royalist cavalry regiments in their quarters before dawn. Then marched on to Cricklade.

Northleach
17 Sept.

16 Sept. Cricklade

17 Sept.

ESSEX

17 Sept. Swindon

18 Sept.

18 Sept. Skirmish at Aldbourne Chase. Then marched to Hungerford.

Aldbourne Chase

18 Sept.

XX
HURRY

17 Sept.
Highworth

XXX
RUPERT

18 Sept.

18 Sept.
Faringdon

XXXX
CHARLES

Wantage

19 Sept.

19 Sept.

20 Sept: Battle of Newbury.

Parliament
Royalist

0   10 miles
0   10 km

N

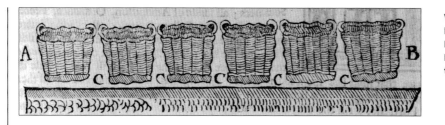

Wicker baskets filled with 'good Earth or Dung' were placed in a line on an earthwork parapet. Musketeers then fired through the gap between each basket.

Majesty's armie can arrive time enough (which he will the presently he receives the answer), he will take up his quarters at or about Wantage, so as to reach Newbury as you propose, but if that cannot be, he is loth to wearie the foot after so great a march as they have had, which you know infers that many are behind'. After a brief halt at Farringdon the army marched on to reach Wantage that evening.

The Parliament army records relate 'on Monday morning our intention being for Hungerford, when the van and body of our army had marched almost all over Auborn [Aldbourne] Chase, there appeared about five or six thousand horse of the enemies, who approached hard to our rereguard, consisting of five regiments of horse, viz: Colonell Middleton's, Lord Gray, Colonell Sheffeild, Harvey and Meldrum's'. Prince Rupert's Royalist cavalry had caught up with the rearguard of the Parliament army. Sir John Byron later described this as an opportunity mishandled as the situation offered 'great advantage for our horse', because 'we were so placed that we had it in our power to both to charge their horse in flank and at the same time to have sent another party to engage their artillery, yet that fair occasion was omitted, and the enemy allowed to join all their forces together, and then we very courageously charged them'.

The Parliament cavalry were outnumbered and forced back on their infantry supports but the action was inconclusive. During this action a French diplomat, the Marquis de Vieuville, accompanying the Royalist army, allowed his enthusiasm to get the better of him and fought as a volunteer with Queen Henrietta Maria's cavalry regiment. De Vieuville was taken prisoner and quarter given him, but as he was marching away with the Lieutenant that had taken him prisoner 'he drew out a pocket pistol and shot him, but proved not mortall, hereupon the Lieutenant with his polax clove his head asunder'.

This action led Essex to try to protect his army's march by crossing over to the other side of the River Kennet before he continued his retreat towards Newbury.

Tuesday 19 September

Essex had sent instructions to Newbury requesting they prepare supplies for his army, and the citizens had made arrangements to provide 'great store of provisions and other necessaries both for horse and man, for the entertainment of his army'. However, as Essex's leading troops arrived in Newbury and his quartermasters were identifying quarters for his soldiers, Royalist cavalry arrived in strength and forced them out of the town.

The cornet (flag) of Sir Samuel Luke's troop of Parliament cavalry. Luke was Scoutmaster General in the Earl of Essex's army. He and his troop joined Essex's army at the general rendezvous at Brackley Heath. The Latin motto *Lex Suprema Salus Patriae* translates as 'The supreme law is the welfare of the country'. (By permission of Partisan Press ECW Picture Library)

THE BATTLE OF NEWBURY

Contemporary Accounts of the Battle

There are four main sources of information on the battle, two Parliament and two Royalist, each written by men who fought in the battle. The Parliament accounts are Sergeant Henry Foster's *A True and Exact Relation of the Marchings of the Two Regiments of the Trained Bands of the City of London* and the official account, written by several (unnamed) colonels of Essex's army, *A True Relation of the Late Expedition of His Excellency, Robert Earle of Essex, for the Relief of Gloucester*. Both accounts were printed in London, Sergeant Foster's account was dated 2 October and the official account was authorised by Parliament on 7 October.

The contemporary historian Thomas May described the official Parliament account with the comment, 'There was punctual Narrative published by some colonels of the parliament-army, gentlemen of great and unstained reputation, concerning this battel, which narrative I have heard some of the enemies confesse to be full not only of modesty but truth in the general, or for the most part.'

The Royalist accounts are *A True and Impartial Relation of the Battaile betwixt His Majesties Army and that of the Rebells neere Newbury in Berkshire* and the manuscript account that Sir John Byron wrote for the Royalist historian the Earl of Clarendon. The first Royalist account was printed from *a Letter from the Army to a Noble Lord* by the Oxford bookseller Leonard Lichfield. The author, thought to be Lord Digby, wrote the letter on 22 September. The second account was that written by Sir John Byron in 1647. Apart from these accounts, the Earl of Clarendon's history provides a useful summary from the perspective of the court at

The Earl of Essex 'gave order for the making of a bridge over the river Severne neere Tewksbury' as a feint before he commenced his retreat. Possibly using the bridging train from Gloucester.

Oxford and every weekly newsbook, both Parliament and Royalist, included reports on the campaign and the battle. In addition there are numerous references in contemporary letters and memoirs.

The Military Position Facing Essex

The Earl of Essex's march had been slowed down to some extent by his baggage train and the heavier cannon (demi-culverins) in his artillery train. He was also hindered by the skirmish at Aldbourne Chase and his decision to cross the River Kennet to place it between him and Prince Rupert's cavalry. By making a forced march, the King's army had reached Newbury before Essex's soldiers could arrive in force, and they now stood astride Essex's route back to his base around London.

When 17th-century armies were this close to one another it was difficult for either army to march away without fighting if its opponent wanted to fight. An army is vulnerable to attack while on the march, and no commander could expect to march away unless his opponent was prepared to let him go. Lord Byron's comments to the Earl of Clarendon illustrate this perspective: 'The Armies were then drawne so near together that it was impossible the enemy could avoid fighting with us if we pleased.' Essex was faced with even greater difficulties than most commanders in this position because the Royalist army was between him and the road back to his base, thereby making difficult any retreat. Essex could consider marching away at night, fooling his opponents by leaving

Colonel's cornet of the Queen's Regiment of Horse. The Queen was French, hence the *fleurs de lys* in the design, and her lifeguard regiment included many French volunteers. The regiment was heavily engaged at the skirmish at Aldbourne Chase. (By permission of Partizan Press ECW Picture Library)

One of the most significant features of the battlefield of Newbury was the series of enclosed fields in the north and centre. Sunken lanes bordered by a bank and hedge were even more of an obstacle, and were as effective as specialist field fortifications.

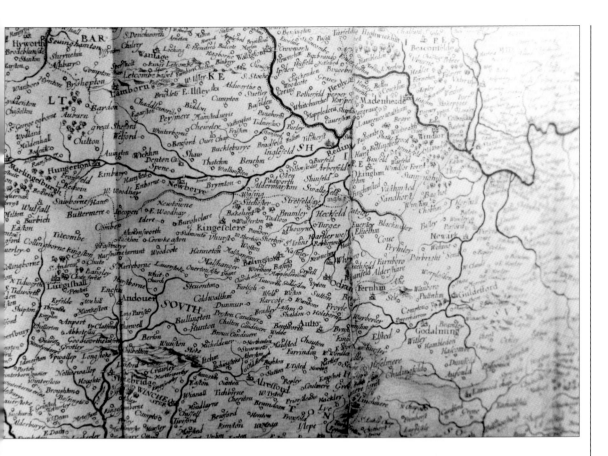

A contemporary plan showing Newbury and the surrounding towns. This map was part of a package published in 1644 by an enterprising London bookseller.

his camp-fires burning, but he would have had to abandon his baggage and heavier artillery pieces if he wanted to outmarch his opponents. Even then, Essex's soldiers had been on poor rations for some days, some were already dropping out on the march, and his army would be under constant threat from Royalist cavalry. In such circumstances a retreat might well mean the destruction of his army.

Essex's Bold Decision

Essex decided to fight and did so with a bold front, appearing confident of victory. He may have had little option except to fight his way out of the trap he had been placed in, but it is a mark of how effective a commander he was that he was able to inspire his men. Essex's army was tired, cold and hungry but they had relieved the siege of Gloucester, which many had thought impossible when the campaign began, and on 15 September they had surprised and captured two Royalist cavalry regiments at Cirencester. Contemporary accounts show that the morale of Essex's soldiers was high as they marched out to fight.

The Battlefield

The battlefield of Newbury lies between two rivers, the Kennet to the north and the Enborne to the south. The battle lines for both armies also run north–south and, for ease of reference, the account in this book will refer to the Northern flank (Parliament left wing and Royalist right wing), the centre, and the Southern flank (Parliament right wing and Royalist left wing). The whole of the battlefield area had narrow lanes

Few buildings survive from the 17th-century town in present-day Newbury.

running across it, and these created a distinctive feature as most were bordered by banks and thick hedges. Narrow lanes restricted the width of any column of soldiers using the lanes and the earth banks and hedges bordering them provided infantry with natural defence lines.

The Northern flank of the battlefield was bounded by the River Kennet, and a series of enclosed fields ran from the river to the centre of the battlefield. These enclosures were small fields surrounded by hedgerows and proved one of the key features of the battlefield. Seventeenth-century armies were trained in formations designed for combat in open countryside; this terrain – small fields and hedgerows – did not suit the military training or the usual battle formations of either side. Infantry units could not fight in this part of the battlefield as they would in open country, and the combat relied more on the use of infantry firepower and light artillery. Cavalry could not be used successfully in this terrain. The Parliament colonels commented in their account that cavalry on this Northern flank 'could not be engaged but in small parties by reason of the hedges'.

The central sector of this battlefield was dominated by rising ground whose high point was referred to in Royalist accounts as a 'round hill'. The Parliament accounts do not use the same term so, presumably, this part of the ridge was more obviously distinct if viewed from the Royalist side. The part of the battlefield where the Royalist army was deployed, and from which they would have seen a 'round hill' in front of them, has now been built over, but modern aerial photography does show a definite round hill. The rising ground becomes steeper towards the centre of the battlefield and would have given a real advantage to whoever could control it. The ground immediately in front of this central point was extremely steep and it would have been difficult for infantry – and even harder for cavalry – to climb it against any kind of opposition. The ground to either side and to the rear of the ridge – where the round hill is the highest point – is steep, but the slope is manageable for both infantry and cavalry. All commanders in this period looked for higher ground because of its obvious advantages in infantry and cavalry combat. High ground was also sought wherever possible as a site on which to place artillery because cannon on higher ground could dominate a battlefield. The importance of the round hill as an artillery position during the battle of Newbury was mentioned in all the Royalist accounts. The Royalist Lord Digby described the high point of the battlefield in a letter written on the day after the battle as 'a round hill from whence a battery could command all the plain before Newbury'. The Royalist weekly newsbook *Mercurius Aulicus* referred to it as a 'little enclosed hill commanding the town of Newbury'. Sir John Byron, who had to attack it with his cavalry during the battle, described the hill as 'full of enclosures and extremely difficult for horse service'.

The Southern flank was bounded by the River Enborne. The terrain from the round hill to the River Enbourne was probably enclosed nearest the round hill, but the main feature on this flank was open country suitable for the usual infantry and cavalry formations of the day. The ground here was a rolling plain, with high points at Bigg's Hill and a slope rising towards a central plateau known as Wash Common. The main strength of the Royalist army, its greatest tactical advantage over its Parliament opponents, was its cavalry, and the open ground on the Southern flank offered the Royalists an opportunity to use their cavalry to its best advantage. Essex was well aware of this threat, and he also knew he would have to make a skilful deployment to oppose it.

The Earl of Clarendon, author of the *History of the Rebellion*, one of the major primary sources for the events of the Civil War.

Essex's Battle Plan

The Earl of Essex was an experienced commander and, in accordance with contemporary practice, would have set out a battle plan before his army marched out on campaign. With a pre-determined plan the army could march in the brigade formations in which it would be deployed for battle. The army could then move easily, brigade by brigade, from its marching formation to its battle formation. During the campaign a commander would adapt his battle plan to take account of any significant changes to the composition of his army such as the addition or subtraction of a significant contingent. In this case, Essex's army was substantially increased at the general rendezvous point at Brackley Heath on 1 September by the addition of provincial regiments and a brigade of London Militia. Although Essex's army had marched in parallel columns for much of this campaign he did have some opportunities to practise deployment in one body during the march – for a review at Brackley Heath, in unusually large brigade formations at Stowe in the Wold and formed up in battle formation in front of Gloucester. However, Essex's original battle plan would have been drawn up for a fight in open country and the terrain he now faced was quite different. Essex and his leading commanders had enough time to look at the battlefield before nightfall on 19 September, and his opening moves before daybreak suggest he made use of the opportunity.

There is no surviving plan of Essex's battle deployment for Newbury. However, several colonels in Essex's army wrote an account of the campaign and the battle, and they took particular care to set out the relative position of Essex's regiments and brigades. They also recorded the names of leading or distinguished officers, writing that 'the officers'

The hollow-Square girdled with shot.

Front.

```
                M M M M • M M M M S
                M M M M • M M M M
                P P P P • P P P P
                P P P P • P P P P
        S
  F  M M M M                                 M M M M
  r  M M M M                                 P P P P
  o  P P P P      D      C      D            P P P P
  n  P P P P                                 P P P P      F
  t                      E                              r
     M M M M                                 P P P P     o
     M M M M                                 M M M M     n
     P P P P      D      L      D            M M M M     t
     P P P P                                 M M M M
                                                   S
                d d d d • d d d d
                d d d d • d d d d
                W W W W • W W W W
                S W W W • W W W W
```

Front.

'The hollow-square girdled with shot' was one of several infantry formations used as defence against cavalry.

names are so particularly exprest in every action, that thou mayest know where to enquire the certainty of every thing'. From this information it is possible to determine the sequence of events that saw them deployed from north to south on the battlefield and the changes as some units were redeployed during the battle. The only Royalist account of the battle to describe the Parliament deployment in any detail describes Essex's right wing with the comment 'they [the Parliament army] had drawne out into Battalia in a little Heath on the South side of Enbourne three bodies of Foot, both lined and flanked with strong bodies of Horse and under favour of Cannon'. A consistent feature of Essex's army at this battle was the number of light artillery pieces, both light cannon and drakes, that were attached to his infantry formation.

Essex deployed the main body of his infantry and a brigade of his cavalry in the Northern and central sections of the battlefield under the command of his Sergeant-Major General, Philip Skippon. Skippon had two infantry brigades, two separate infantry regiments, a 'Forlorn Hope' of 'commanded musketeers', the army's heavy artillery, including at least two demi-culverins, and the army's reserve, which comprised the London Trained Bands and Auxiliaries. Essex personally commanded the right wing with a force consisting of some of his best cavalry supported by three bodies of infantry, which was made up of his own (strong) infantry regiment and the infantry brigades commanded by Colonel Harry Barclay and Colonel James Holborne. Essex's right wing was more of a small army in itself than the usual wing of an army, which typically comprised cavalry and 'commanded' musketeers, and was intended to hold the Southern flank of the battlefield against Prince Rupert's Royalist cavalry.

The Parliament field word was 'Religion' and the field sign a green 'bough' worn in their hats. One account says the field signs were taken from 'furze [gorse] and broom', plants commonly found growing on heathland throughout England.

The Royalist Battle Plan

The Royalist army would also have marched away from their base around Evesham with a set battle plan. However, they would not have been able to use theirs at Newbury any more than Essex could use his because the ground did not suit mainstream contemporary tactics. There is no surviving Royalist battle plan for this action and from comments by both Clarendon and Sir John Byron it is possible that there never was a complete plan for this battle because the Royalist high command didn't intend to fight one. Clarendon wrote that 'it was resolved over night not to engage in battle but upon such grounds as should give an assurance of victory'. However, Clarendon went on to write that 'contrary to this resolution, when the earl of Essex had with excellent conduct drawn out his army in battalia upon a hill called Bigg's Hill, within less than a mile of the town, and ordered his men in all places to the best advantage, by the precipitate courage of some young officers, who had good commands, and who unhappily undervalued the courage of the enemy, strong parties became successively so far engaged that the King was compelled to put the whole to hazard of a battle, and to give the enemy at least an equal game to play'. Sir John Byron commented, in a long list of mistakes which he considered that Prince Rupert had made, 'and hereupon a fourth error may be observed, for notwithstanding the necessity there was of fighting (at least if they [Essex's army] persisted in their marching to London and we in ours of preventing them) yet no orders were given out for the manner of our fighting and how the army should be embattled as usually is done on the like occasions'.

There is no comparable Royalist account to the official Parliament account. The Oxford Royalist account only provides general information and concentrates on two key points, the struggle for control of the round

The 'round hill' at Newbury. A view from the west 'Parliament' side showing a sloping hill. It was not exceptionally steep, but it was a clear advantage for any defending force.

The 'round hill' at Newbury. The top of the plateau is relatively flat and well drained, good ground to manoeuvre infantry or deploy artillery.

hill in the centre and Prince Rupert's cavalry action on the Southern flank. The most detailed Royalist account is that of Sir John Byron, which details his actions in the centre. However, as Byron said himself, 'What was done upon the Heath [the Southern flank], where the main body of our horse and foot fought, I will not relate, because I was not an eye-witness of it.' This makes any reconstruction of the Royalist deployment very difficult. However, it is possible to determine where the major concentrations of troops were made from comments by Sir John Byron and the Earl of Clarendon, and from Parliamentary accounts of the type and concentration of Royalist troops that they fought.

Sir John Byron recorded that 'my brigade of horse had the van and about 5 in the morning I had orders to march towards a little hill full of enclosures, which the enemy (through the negligence before mentioned) had possessed himself of'. By the term 'van' Byron meant the vanguard of cavalry that marched at the head of the army and usually formed its right wing cavalry when deployed. Byron said: '[My] orders were, only with my own and Sir Thos Aston's regiment to draw behind the commanded foot led by Lord Wentworth and Col. George Lisle, and should be ready to second them, in case the enemy's horse should advance towards them: the rest of my brigade was by Prince Rupert commanded to the Heath.' Parliament accounts refer to Essex's wing of the army, which opposed Prince Rupert's left wing, facing attack from Royalist cavalry and substantial numbers of infantry. The Parliament's Sergeant Henry Foster referred to the Royalists having a battery of 'eight pieces of ordnance' on high ground close to the present-day Falkland monument.

Overall, the accounts suggest that Prince Rupert led out increasing numbers of troops to fight in the open ground to the south. This force finally consisted of most of his cavalry (four brigades) and formed bodies of infantry. Sir John Byron referred to this force as 'the main body of our horse and foot', so Prince Rupert evidently had a substantial body of infantry. The Royalist army probably had four brigades of infantry at Newbury, of these Sir Nicholas Byron's fought in the centre and Sir William

Vavasour's fought on the Northern flank. The remaining two infantry brigades (commanded by John Belasyse and Sir Gilbert Gerard) are likely to have served with Prince Rupert on the Southern flank. The Royalist heavy artillery was placed on high ground near the present-day Falkland monument. Sir John Byron with his two remaining regiments of horse, Sir Nicholas Byron's infantry brigade and about 1,000 'commanded' musketeers under Lord Wentworth and Sir George Lisle fought in the centre. Sir William Vavasour's infantry brigade, deployed on the northern flank, consisted of Welsh regiments raised by Lord Herbert and a contingent from the Worcester garrison.

There is no reference to a Royalist field word for the day in any Royalist account. The Parliament soldier Sergeant Henry Foster wrote 'theirs [the Royalist field word] was Queen Mary in the field'. Queen Mary used in this sense was probably a reference to the Queen, Henrietta Maria.

THE BATTLE BEGINS

Essex and his leading officers evidently took the time to study the ground while daylight allowed on 19 September, because the Parliament army moved out early the next morning with a clear plan in mind. Essex may have received useful intelligence from some of the many Parliament sympathisers in Newbury, but his opening moves for the day show a military appreciation of the advantages of gaining control of the high ground. His targets would be the ridge that ended in the round hill in the centre of the battlefield and, on the Southern flank, Bigg's Hill followed by the plateau on Wash Common. Essex had divided his army into two groups, each comprising infantry, cavalry and artillery. His infantry commander, Sergeant-Major General Philip Skippon, led the main body of the infantry with its supporting light artillery, Colonel John Middleton's brigade of cavalry and the army's heavy artillery. Essex, who himself led a separate group comprised of infantry with supporting light artillery and the best of his cavalry, was the first to move that morning, making a very early start. Sergeant Foster recorded that 'very early before day, we had drawn up all our army in their several regiments, and marched away by break of day', and the Parliament official account recorded that 'by breake of day order was given for our march [Essex's wing of the army] to an hill called Big's-hill neere to Newbury'.

The Royalists had also made preparations to fight on 19 September. The Oxford Royalist account recorded that 'consultation was held of the way to prevent their further evading us, and it was resolved on for the best, to draw all the King's Army that night [19th September] into a large field on the other side of Newbury' [i.e. outside the town itself and between the Parliament army and the town]. This ensured that the Royalist infantry would be in place and ready for deployment early the following morning, a precaution against a surprise attack. Royalist cavalry were active overnight and there were some small skirmishes with Parliament cavalry outposts. By morning a small detachment of Royalist cavalry were posted at 'Biggs Hill' but the Royalist army neglected to make as careful a survey of the battlefield as their Parliament opponents and, as Lord Byron commented, 'here another error was committed, and that a most gross and absurd one, in not viewing the ground, though

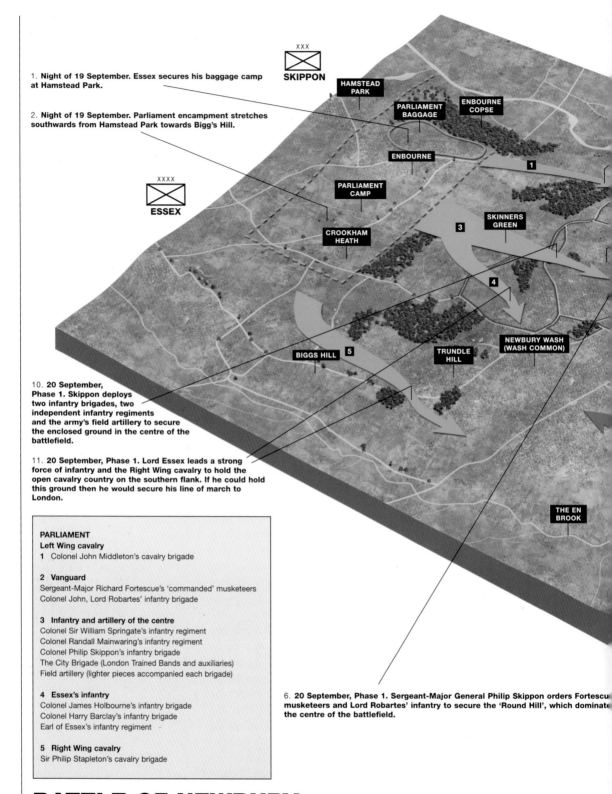

XXX
SKIPPON

1. **Night of 19 September.** Essex secures his baggage camp at Hamstead Park.

2. **Night of 19 September.** Parliament encampment stretches southwards from Hamstead Park towards Bigg's Hill.

XXXX
ESSEX

HAMSTEAD PARK

PARLIAMENT BAGGAGE

ENBOURNE COPSE

ENBOURNE

1

PARLIAMENT CAMP

SKINNERS GREEN

3

CROOKHAM HEATH

4

NEWBURY WASH (WASH COMMON)

BIGGS HILL **5**

TRUNDLE HILL

THE EN BROOK

10. **20 September, Phase 1.** Skippon deploys two infantry brigades, two independent infantry regiments and the army's field artillery to secure the enclosed ground in the centre of the battlefield.

11. **20 September, Phase 1.** Lord Essex leads a strong force of infantry and the Right Wing cavalry to hold the open cavalry country on the southern flank. If he could hold this ground then he would secure his line of march to London.

PARLIAMENT
Left Wing cavalry
1 Colonel John Middleton's cavalry brigade

2 Vanguard
Sergeant-Major Richard Fortescue's 'commanded' musketeers
Colonel John, Lord Robartes' infantry brigade

3 Infantry and artillery of the centre
Colonel Sir William Springate's infantry regiment
Colonel Randall Mainwaring's infantry regiment
Colonel Philip Skippon's infantry brigade
The City Brigade (London Trained Bands and auxiliaries)
Field artillery (lighter pieces accompanied each brigade)

4 Essex's infantry
Colonel James Holbourne's infantry brigade
Colonel Harry Barclay's infantry brigade
Earl of Essex's infantry regiment

5 Right Wing cavalry
Sir Philip Stapleton's cavalry brigade

6. **20 September, Phase 1.** Sergeant-Major General Philip Skippon orders Fortescu musketeers and Lord Robartes' infantry to secure the 'Round Hill', which dominate the centre of the battlefield.

BATTLE OF NEWBURY
19–20 September 1643, viewed from the south-east showing the two armies marching out of camp to deploy as the struggle for the key feature of the 'Round Hill' is already underway in the centre.

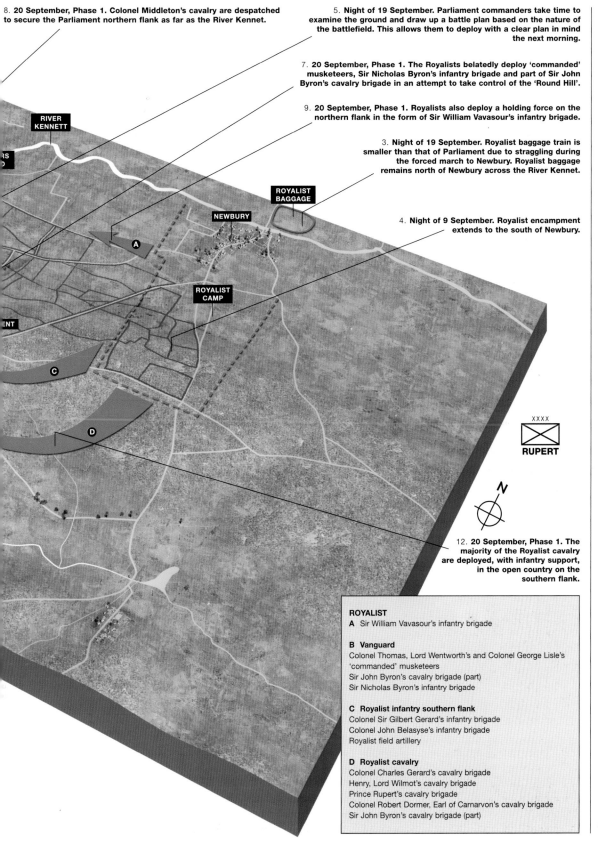

8. **20 September, Phase 1. Colonel Middleton's cavalry are despatched to secure the Parliament northern flank as far as the River Kennet.**

5. **Night of 19 September. Parliament commanders take time to examine the ground and draw up a battle plan based on the nature of the battlefield. This allows them to deploy with a clear plan in mind the next morning.**

7. **20 September, Phase 1. The Royalists belatedly deploy 'commanded' musketeers, Sir Nicholas Byron's infantry brigade and part of Sir John Byron's cavalry brigade in an attempt to take control of the 'Round Hill'.**

9. **20 September, Phase 1. Royalists also deploy a holding force on the northern flank in the form of Sir William Vavasour's infantry brigade.**

3. **Night of 19 September. Royalist baggage train is smaller than that of Parliament due to straggling during the forced march to Newbury. Royalist baggage remains north of Newbury across the River Kennet.**

4. **Night of 9 September. Royalist encampment extends to the south of Newbury.**

RIVER KENNETT

NEWBURY

ROYALIST BAGGAGE

ROYALIST CAMP

A

C

D

xxxx

RUPERT

N

12. **20 September, Phase 1. The majority of the Royalist cavalry are deployed, with infantry support, in the open country on the southern flank.**

ROYALIST
A Sir William Vavasour's infantry brigade

B Vanguard
Colonel Thomas, Lord Wentworth's and Colonel George Lisle's 'commanded' musketeers
Sir John Byron's cavalry brigade (part)
Sir Nicholas Byron's infantry brigade

C Royalist infantry southern flank
Colonel Sir Gilbert Gerard's infantry brigade
Colonel John Belasyse's infantry brigade
Royalist field artillery

D Royalist cavalry
Colonel Charles Gerard's cavalry brigade
Henry, Lord Wilmot's cavalry brigade
Prince Rupert's cavalry brigade
Colonel Robert Dormer, Earl of Carnarvon's cavalry brigade
Sir John Byron's cavalry brigade (part)

we had day enough [daylight enough] to have done it, and not possessing ourselves of those hills above the town by which the enemy was necessarily to march the next day to Reading'. The Oxford Royalist account made a similar comment that there was 'within the Enemies Dominion a round hill not observed by us the night before'.

The battle began with Essex's advance on Bigg's Hill to secure the advantage of rising ground on the open Southern flank. Essex's force consisted of 'his owne regiment, Colonell Barclay's [Barclay's, Holmstead's and Tyrrell's regiments] and Colonell Holborn's [Holborne's, Thompson's and Langham's regiments] brigades and the best of his cavalry [Essex's lifeguard troop, Essex's own regiment, the regiments of Colonels John Dalbier, Sir James Ramsey, Edmund Harvey, Arthur Goodwin, Richard Norton and three commanded troops under Sir Samuel Luke]'. Skippon's advance must have commenced at about the same time. The official Parliament account recorded that 'Major Generall Skippon in the morning, when his Excellency [Essex] was ingaged upon the hill [the Southern flank], hastened to the top of the hill [the round hill in the centre], where our vanguard was in fight, having before ordered the march of our train of artillerie'. From this vantage point Skippon 'perceived a great strength of the enemy both horse and foot in divers great bodies advancing' and then decided how best to deploy his men. Skippon's force consisted of Colonel Lord Robartes' Brigade (Lord Robartes', Sir William Constable's, Francis Martin's regiments), his own brigade (Philip Skippon's, Sir William Brooke's, Henry Bulstrode's regiments), Sir William Springate's Regiment, Randall Mainwaring's Regiment, Sergeant-Major Richard Fortescue's 'Forlorn Hope' of commanded musketeers and a reserve of the Red and the Blue Trained Bands and the Red, Blue and Orange regiments of London Auxiliaries. Skippon also had the remainder of Essex's cavalry for support, the army's heavy artillery and a large number of light artillery pieces.

Skippon's leading units, Sergeant-Major Richard Fortescue's commanded musketeers and Lord Robartes' Brigade, secured the ground in the centre while Skippon deployed his army from its marching columns to its battle formation. Morale was high and Sergeant Foster recorded the London Trained Bands, which formed the reserve, 'advancing towards the enemy with the most cheerful and couragious spirits'. In front of them 'The Lord Robart's souldiers had begun to skirmish with them [the Royalists] before we came up to the enemy; which we hearing, put us to a running march till wee sweat again, hastening to their reliefe and succour.'

The Royalists had also been up early in the morning. Sir John Byron recorded that 'about 5 in the morning I had orders to march towards a little hill full of enclosures, which the enemy (through the negligence before mentioned) had possessed himself of and had brought up two small field pieces and was bringing up more'. Sir John Byron was supported by Sir Nicholas Byron's infantry brigade and commanded musketeers under Sir George Lisle but, as Sir John Byron recorded, 'the commanded foot … were not able to make good the place.' The Royalist's initial attack had failed to take the Parliament position. This was probably the action against Lord Robartes Brigade where 'my Lord Robarts his brigade with four or five small peeces just where the enemy advanced, who gave them so warm an entertainment that they ran shamefully: and my Lord Robarts possest the ground which the enemy came first unto; his Lieutenant colonell was shot in the face.'

THE SECOND STAGE

By a swift march Essex had gained the advantage of the ground on the battlefield both in the centre around the round hill and at Bigg's Hill. Essex's army was now deployed to fight in a position of advantage, but it was short of rations and the best strategy of their Royalist opponents was not to attack Essex but to wait him out. Essex's soldiers would be at a disadvantage if he tried to march away, and his army could be attacked in its marching formation.

Instead, the Royalist army mounted a series of attacks on Essex's position throughout the day. The Royalist courtier and historian, the Earl of Clarendon, suggested that 'by the precipitate courage of some young officers who had good commands, and who unhappily always undervalued the courage of the enemy, strong parties became successively so far engaged that the King was compelled to put the whole of the hazard of a battle, and to give the enemy at least an equal game to play'. In other words, a series of small actions quickly escalated and the whole Royalist army became committed to a battle it did not need to fight. The Oxford Royalist account suggested that Essex deliberately suckered them in, commenting that Essex's deployment on the Southern flank was intended 'in some sort to lead on' Prince Rupert to commence the battle by attacking Essex's position with the 'tempting prospect of that little Battalia I mentioned upon the Heath'.

The Southern Flank

The account of the cavalry action to the south bears out Clarendon's comment of a steadily escalating series of actions. The official Parliament account described the whole of the cavalry action in one piece: 'The actions of our horse thus described wholly (because we were loth to interrupt the series, for the reader's clearer understanding).' The Oxford Royalist account is much briefer but clearly describes the same action.

The Parliament cavalry evidently used a narrow lane to advance past Bigg's Hill and their leading regiment had time to deploy onto open ground before the Royalist cavalry attacked them. The Parliament cavalry followed the Dutch tactic of waiting to receive an attack and firing just before their charging opponents reached them. At Edgehill the strain of waiting had been too much for newly raised soldiers, and the Parliament cavalry had fired at long distance then turned and ran. At Newbury they stood their ground, the front line cavalrymen firing the first of their two pistols at the last minute, and the tactic was successful in beating off the first Royalist assault. The Parliament cavalry commander, Sir Philip Stapleton, pursued the Royalists back to their own starting point, and was then able to rally his men and fall back and re-form ready to fight again. This initial action gave the remainder of Stapleton's cavalry brigade time to debouch out of the lane and deploy in battle formation. This was probably the point at which Essex formed the infantry and cavalry of this wing into a

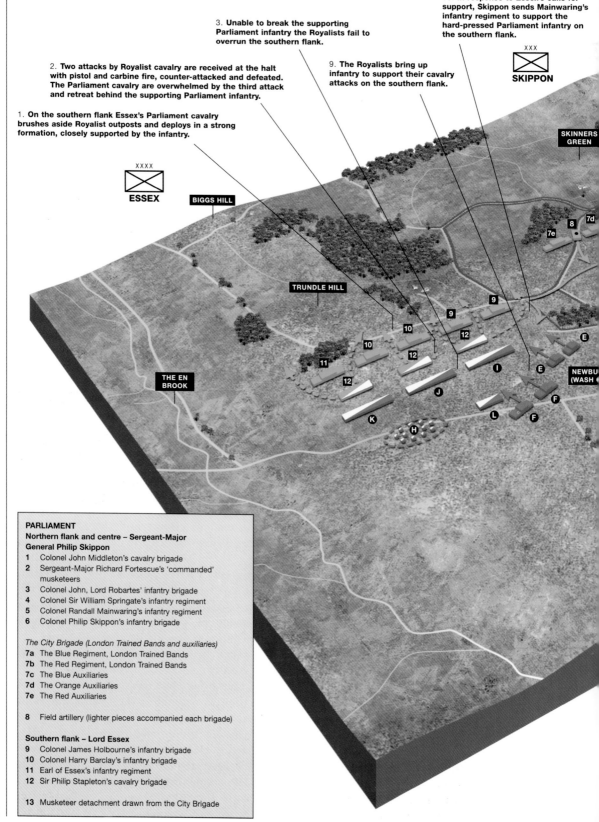

10. **In response to Essex's calls for support, Skippon sends Mainwaring's infantry regiment to support the hard-pressed Parliament infantry on the southern flank.**

3. **Unable to break the supporting Parliament infantry the Royalists fail to overrun the southern flank.**

2. **Two attacks by Royalist cavalry are received at the halt with pistol and carbine fire, counter-attacked and defeated. The Parliament cavalry are overwhelmed by the third attack and retreat behind the supporting Parliament infantry.**

9. **The Royalists bring up infantry to support their cavalry attacks on the southern flank.**

1. **On the southern flank Essex's Parliament cavalry brushes aside Royalist outposts and deploys in a strong formation, closely supported by the infantry.**

XXX
SKIPPON

XXXX
ESSEX

BIGGS HILL

SKINNERS GREEN

7d
8
7e

TRUNDLE HILL

9
9
9

E

10
10
12
12
E

11
12
12
I
E

THE EN BROOK

J
L
F

K
F

NEWBU (WASH

H

PARLIAMENT
**Northern flank and centre – Sergeant-Major
General Philip Skippon**
1 Colonel John Middleton's cavalry brigade
2 Sergeant-Major Richard Fortescue's 'commanded'
    musketeers
3 Colonel John, Lord Robartes' infantry brigade
4 Colonel Sir William Springate's infantry regiment
5 Colonel Randall Mainwaring's infantry regiment
6 Colonel Philip Skippon's infantry brigade

The City Brigade (London Trained Bands and auxiliaries)
7a The Blue Regiment, London Trained Bands
7b The Red Regiment, London Trained Bands
7c The Blue Auxiliaries
7d The Orange Auxiliaries
7e The Red Auxiliaries

8 Field artillery (lighter pieces accompanied each brigade)

Southern flank – Lord Essex
9   Colonel James Holbourne's infantry brigade
10 Colonel Harry Barclay's infantry brigade
11 Earl of Essex's infantry regiment
12 Sir Philip Stapleton's cavalry brigade

13 Musketeer detachment drawn from the City Brigade

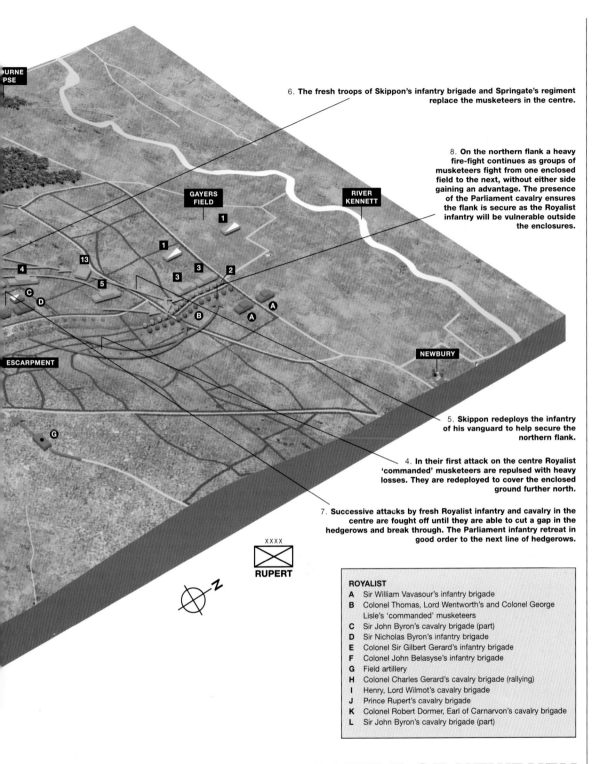

6. The fresh troops of Skippon's infantry brigade and Springate's regiment replace the musketeers in the centre.

8. On the northern flank a heavy fire-fight continues as groups of musketeers fight from one enclosed field to the next, without either side gaining an advantage. The presence of the Parliament cavalry ensures the flank is secure as the Royalist infantry will be vulnerable outside the enclosures.

URNE PSE

GAYERS FIELD

RIVER KENNETT

ESCARPMENT

NEWBURY

5. Skippon redeploys the infantry of his vanguard to help secure the northern flank.

4. In their first attack on the centre Royalist 'commanded' musketeers are repulsed with heavy losses. They are redeployed to cover the enclosed ground further north.

7. Successive attacks by fresh Royalist infantry and cavalry in the centre are fought off until they are able to cut a gap in the hedgerows and break through. The Parliament infantry retreat in good order to the next line of hedgerows.

XXXX

RUPERT

ROYALIST
A Sir William Vavasour's infantry brigade
B Colonel Thomas, Lord Wentworth's and Colonel George Lisle's 'commanded' musketeers
C Sir John Byron's cavalry brigade (part)
D Sir Nicholas Byron's infantry brigade
E Colonel Sir Gilbert Gerard's infantry brigade
F Colonel John Belasyse's infantry brigade
G Field artillery
H Colonel Charles Gerard's cavalry brigade (rallying)
I Henry, Lord Wilmot's cavalry brigade
J Prince Rupert's cavalry brigade
K Colonel Robert Dormer, Earl of Carnarvon's cavalry brigade
L Sir John Byron's cavalry brigade (part)

BATTLE OF NEWBURY

20 September 1643, viewed from the south-east. In the second phase of the battle, on the southern flank the Royalist cavalry clash with the Parliament cavalry while in the centre Royalist cavalry and infantry struggle to come to grips with the Parliament infantry. An inconclusive fire-fight continues between units of musketeers on the northern flank.

Lucius Cary, Lord Falkland, King Charles' Secretary of State. He was killed at Newbury while fighting as a volunteer with Sir John Byron's cavalry brigade.

battle formation that was described in the Oxford Royalist account as 'three bodies of Foot, both lined and flanked with strong bodies of Horse'.

Essex's formation fought off a second Royalist cavalry attack, but a third attack in greater numbers broke the Parliament cavalry. Essex's lifeguard troop and his own cavalry regiment had now fired both their pistols, one in each of the previous two attacks and, under attack in front and flank, was forced back on the entrance of the lane from which they had originally deployed. Their supporting infantry were forced back but not broken, and those Royalist cavalry who pursued Sir Philip Stapleton's troopers and 'entred the lane with ours were most of them slaine'. The Parliament official account commented that 'Captain Abercromy, and Captain Shibborne … with their dragoones' behaved very gallantly and this may indicate that the Parliament dragoons were placed in the hedgerows and ambushed the pursuing Royalists.

The Oxford Royalist account recorded 'the issue of the Battell on the heath (first begun and quickly ended) was a total routing of their horse, the possessing of five pieces of Cannon there, though able to bring off but one of them, the forcing of the foot to retreat into their strength, though unbroken for (give them their due) they shewed themselves like good men'. Clarendon's account was similar: 'The King's horse with a kind of contempt for the enemy, charged with wonderful boldness upon all grounds of inequality, and were so far too hard for the troops on the other side that they routed them in most places, till they had left the greatest part of their foot without any guard at all of horse. But then the foot behaved themselves admirably on the enemy's part, and gave their scattered horse time to rally.'

Essentially, this meant the Royalist cavalry had finally been able to defeat the Parliament cavalry, but because the Royalists could not break the supporting Parliament infantry they could not overrun Essex's southern flank.

The Centre

The Royalist commanded musketeers had failed to make any headway against the Parliament infantry and supporting light artillery in the centre. Sir Nicholas Byron's infantry brigade came up in support because 'the commanded musketeers not being able to make good the place' and mounted a further attack 'with part of the regiment of guards [The King's Lifeguard] and Sir Michael Woodhouse's and my Lord Gerard's regiments of foot … but the service grew so hot, that in a very short time, of twelve ensigns that marched up with my Lord Gerard's regiment, eleven were brought off the field hurt and Ned Villiers [Lieutenant-Colonel of Lord Gerard's regiment] shot through the shoulder. Upon this a confusion was heard amongst the foot, calling horse! horse! Whereupon I [Sir John Byron] advanced with those two regiments I had [Sir John Byron's and Sir Thomas Aston's] and commanded them to halt while I went to view the ground, and to see what way there was to that place where the enemy's foot were drawn up, which I found to be enclosed with a high quick [thick] hedge and no passage into it, but by a narrow gap through which but one horse at a time could go and that not without difficulty.'

CASUALTIES OF COLONEL CHARLES GERARD'S REGIMENT AT NEWBURY

Royalist Return of the wounded officers and men of Colonel Charles Gerard's regiment at Newbury: 1 Lieutenant-Colonel, 2 Captains, 4 Lieutenants, 9 Ensigns, 7 Sergeants, 79 'common soldiers'.

Two of the 11 Ensigns mentioned above probably served with a smaller Royalist contingent serving alongside Colonel Gerard's regiment. The casualty figures for Charles Gerard's regiment demonstrate that Civil War officers led from the front.

Sir John Byron was giving orders 'for making the gapp wide enough … [when] my horse was shott in the throat with a musket bullet and his bit broken in his mouth so that I was forced to call for another horse, in the meanwhile my Lord Falkland [Lucius Cary, Viscount Falkland, Secretary of State, riding with Sir John Byron's own troop as a volunteer that day] (more gallantly than advisedly) spurred his horse through the gapp, where he and his horse were immediately killed. The passage being then made somewhat wide, and I now having another horse, drew in my troop first, giving orders for the rest to follow, and charged the enemy, who entertained us with a great salvo of musket shott, and discharged their two drakes upon us, laden with case shott, which killed some and hurt many of my men, so that we were forced to wheel off and could not meet them at that charge.'

Once Byron's men had made a larger entrance in the hedge, Skippon's Parliament infantry fell back to the other side of the close, taking their light artillery with them. Byron's cavalry followed them up to 'where they had the advantage of a hedge at their backs, and poured in another volley of shott upon us, when Sir Thomas Ashton's horse was killed under him, and withal kept us off so with their pikes we could not break them, but were forced to wheel off again, they in the meantime retreating into another little close.' Byron then commented that, 'Our [Royalist] foot then drew upon the ground from whence we had beaten the enemy, and kept it, and drew the horse back to the former station; for this service I lost near upon a hundred horse and men out of my regiment, whereof out of my own troop twenty-six.'

Skippon's Parliament infantry were still able to control the central feature, the round hill, and he retained the City Brigade as his reserve (two regiments of Trained Bands and three of auxiliaries).

The Northern Flank

None of the authors of the four main accounts was involved in the fighting on this flank. However, there is one contemporary account by an unknown Royalist cavalry officer who was ordered to check the position on this flank later in the day and 'found Sir William Vavasour there with his brigade'.

The Parliament official account states that Skippon made a strong deployment on this flank, moving his leading units – Sergeant-Major Richard Fortescue's 'Forlorn Hope' of 'commanded' musketeers and Colonel Robartes' brigade – from the centre to the Northern flank together with Colonel John Middleton's cavalry brigade. Skippon evidently reinforced Major Fortescue's detachment with musketeers from the London Trained Bands, as Sergeant Foster recorded that 'we had sixty

77

ROYALIST AND PARLIAMENT CAVALRY CLASH ON THE SOUTHERN FLANK AT NEWBURY (pages 78–79)

The Earl of Essex led out a strong force of cavalry, infantry and light artillery to fight in the open country of the southern flank at Newbury, leaving his Sergeant-Major General Philip Skippon with a separate force to hold the enclosed ground in the centre and on the northern flank. The Parliament cavalry had been overwhelmed at the battle of Edgehill the previous year and the Royalist cavalry commanders believed that Parliament cavalry would not be able to stand against them. At Newbury the Parliament cavalry deployed on the southern flank under Sir Philip Stapleton proved them wrong. The tactics used by the two sides were different; the Parliament cavalry were drawn up six deep and waited to receive an attack at the halt, firing pistols and carbines at close range to break up enemy formations then counterattacking. The Royalists used a shallower deployment, only three deep, and sought to sweep their opponents away with a furious charge. At Edgehill this Royalist tactic had been successful against trained but inexperienced Parliament cavalry, whose nerve broke in the face of waves of enemy cavalry charging towards them. At Newbury, however, the Parliament cavalry showed they had learnt from the experience and used their tactic of receiving the charge at the halt with pistol and carbine fire to break the first two Royalist cavalry attacks before finally being overwhelmed by superior numbers. Prince Rupert, the Royalist commander on the southern flank, was unable to follow up this success by turning the Parliament army's flank because he was unable to break the supporting Parliament infantry drawn up behind their

cavalry. Once two bodies of cavalry meet whatever formation they use breaks up and then it is every man for himself in a desperate melee. Here we see that stage of the struggle as Parliament and Royalist cavalrymen fight hand-to-hand. Neither side wear uniforms but they are distinguished from one another by the colour of their sashes – red for the King and orange for Parliament. There are other distinctions between the two sides as most of the equipment of the Parliament cavalry was manufactured locally and they wear English tri-bar cavalry helmets and carry 'English-lock' flintlock pistols. Their Royalist opponents wear European single bar *zischagge* helmets bought from Holland, the centre of the international arms trade of the day. Note the Parliament cavalryman (1) angles his pistol as he fires so that the priming pan is uppermost. By doing so he ensures that the priming powder is concentrated over the touch-hole, making it more likely that it will ignite the main charge and fire the pistol when he pulls the trigger. The Royalist cavalryman (2) is using a poleaxe, a weapon with an axe-blade on one side and a spike on the other. The spike was intended to punch through armour. This weapon was designed for use against men wearing full cavalry armour and was not part of the formal equipment issued to arquebusiers, the main class of cavalry used by both sides. However, the poleaxe was a versatile and deadly weapon and cavalrymen on both sides are known to have carried them. The Parliament cavalryman (3) is wearing a bridle gauntlet, its aim being to prevent an opponent hacking into his left arm in the melee. The cavalry flag (cornet) (4) is that of Colonel Richard Norton's troop. (Graham Turner)

files of muskettiers drawn off for the forlorn hope who were ingaged against the enemy in the field upon our left flank'. Skippon's objective was to secure 'the high way that came from Newbury just upon us' and which also led directly to Hamstead Park where the Parliamentary baggage train was parked. The Parliament official account describes this deployment as follows: 'Major Generall Skippon placed [Fortescue's Forlorn Hope] on the left of my Lord Roberts his brigade, upon the high way that came from Newbury just upon us, upon which way four drakes were likewise placed, and well defenced; though the enemies came up so close, that they took away a limmer [limber] of one of our peeces, but it was with the losse of many of their lives. Colonell Mannering's regiment was placed on the right hand between the hill and my Lord Roberts his brigade.'

THE THIRD STAGE

The Southern Flank

After Stapleton's cavalry had been beaten off the field they rallied behind their supporting infantry. However, although Essex's infantry came under severe pressure, being 'hotly charged by the enemie's horse and foot', the best that Prince Rupert could do was drive them back onto Bigg's Hill. The Royalists needed to break the Parliament infantry to gain a victory but they failed to do so. After 'four hours upon very hot service' Essex called for reinforcements from Skippon.

Skippon may still have been doubtful about the fighting ability of the Militia regiments that formed his reserve, as he recalled Colonel Mainwaring's regiment from the Northern flank, taking a regiment from the reserve, the Blue Auxiliaries, to replace it. However, 'it fortuned that his regiment [Mainwaring's] was no sooner brought on, but they were overcharged with two great bodies of horse and foot so, that they were forced to retreat and lose that ground that the fore-named forces had gotten. which Colonell Holborne perceiving with his brigade gave the enemy a round salvo, and instantly his own and Colonell Barclay's brigades and his Excellency's regiment again advancing beat back the enemy, regaind the ground.'

Once Mainwaring's regiment was forced back there appears to have been a weak point at the junction between Essex's and Skippon's sections of the Parliament army. Prince Rupert was evidently preparing to exploit this weak point when Skippon called out the two best regiments in his reserve, the Red and the Blue Regiments of the London Trained Bands to fill the gap. Sergeant Foster recorded that 'our two regiments of the trained bands were placed in open campania upon the right wing of the whole army [i.e. Skippon's portion of it]. The enemy had there planted eight pieces of ordnance, and stood in a great body of horse and foot, wee being placed right opposite against them, and far lesse than twice musket shot distance from them. They began their battery against us with their great guns, above halfe an houre before we could get any of our guns up to us.'

The London Trained Bands were in a difficult position as they stood out in the open under artillery fire from the Royalist battery (sited approximately where the Falkland monument stands today). The Londoners were also under continuous attack from Royalist cavalry and infantry. At first the two regiments were deployed separately with the Blue

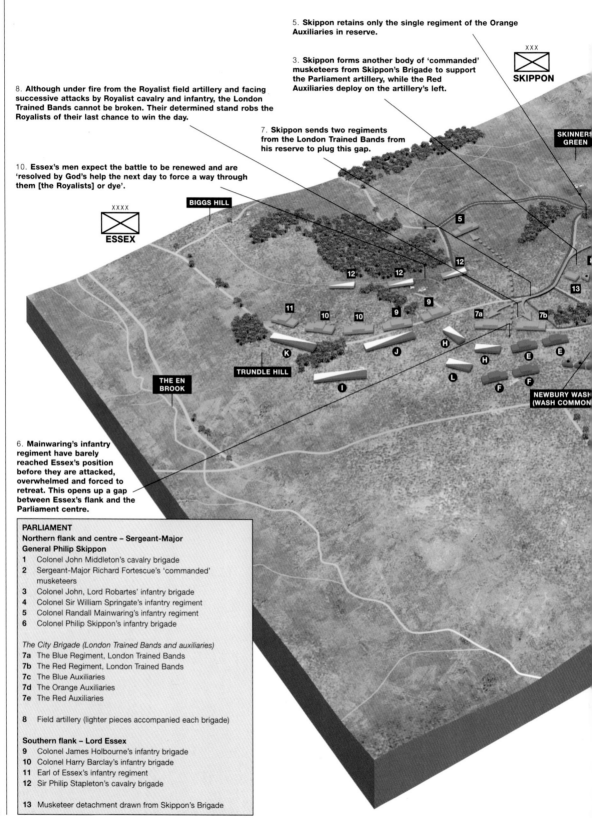

5. Skippon retains only the single regiment of the Orange Auxiliaries in reserve.

3. Skippon forms another body of 'commanded' musketeers from Skippon's Brigade to support the Parliament artillery, while the Red Auxiliaries deploy on the artillery's left.

8. Although under fire from the Royalist field artillery and facing successive attacks by Royalist cavalry and infantry, the London Trained Bands cannot be broken. Their determined stand robs the Royalists of their last chance to win the day.

7. Skippon sends two regiments from the London Trained Bands from his reserve to plug this gap.

10. Essex's men expect the battle to be renewed and are 'resolved by God's help the next day to force a way through them [the Royalists] or dye'.

6. Mainwaring's infantry regiment have barely reached Essex's position before they are attacked, overwhelmed and forced to retreat. This opens up a gap between Essex's flank and the Parliament centre.

SKIPPON

SKINNERS GREEN

ESSEX

BIGGS HILL

TRUNDLE HILL

THE EN BROOK

NEWBURY WASH (WASH COMMON)

PARLIAMENT
Northern flank and centre – Sergeant-Major
General Philip Skippon
1   Colonel John Middleton's cavalry brigade
2   Sergeant-Major Richard Fortescue's 'commanded' musketeers
3   Colonel John, Lord Robartes' infantry brigade
4   Colonel Sir William Springate's infantry regiment
5   Colonel Randall Mainwaring's infantry regiment
6   Colonel Philip Skippon's infantry brigade

The City Brigade (London Trained Bands and auxiliaries)
7a The Blue Regiment, London Trained Bands
7b The Red Regiment, London Trained Bands
7c The Blue Auxiliaries
7d The Orange Auxiliaries
7e The Red Auxiliaries

8   Field artillery (lighter pieces accompanied each brigade)

Southern flank – Lord Essex
9   Colonel James Holbourne's infantry brigade
10 Colonel Harry Barclay's infantry brigade
11 Earl of Essex's infantry regiment
12 Sir Philip Stapleton's cavalry brigade

13 Musketeer detachment drawn from Skippon's Brigade

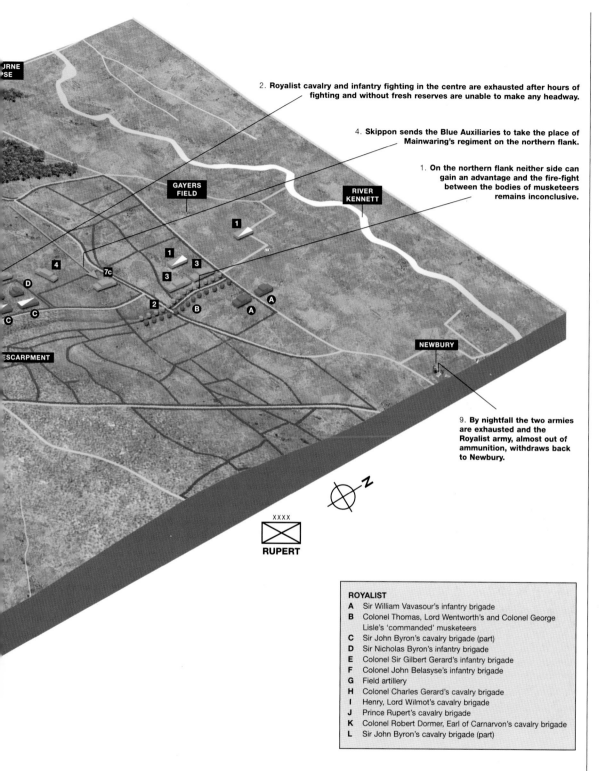

2. Royalist cavalry and infantry fighting in the centre are exhausted after hours of fighting and without fresh reserves are unable to make any headway.

4. Skippon sends the Blue Auxiliaries to take the place of Mainwaring's regiment on the northern flank.

1. On the northern flank neither side can gain an advantage and the fire-fight between the bodies of musketeers remains inconclusive.

9. By nightfall the two armies are exhausted and the Royalist army, almost out of ammunition, withdraws back to Newbury.

GAYERS FIELD

RIVER KENNETT

ESCARPMENT

NEWBURY

RUPERT

N

ROYALIST
A   Sir William Vavasour's infantry brigade
B   Colonel Thomas, Lord Wentworth's and Colonel George Lisle's 'commanded' musketeers
C   Sir John Byron's cavalry brigade (part)
D   Sir Nicholas Byron's infantry brigade
E   Colonel Sir Gilbert Gerard's infantry brigade
F   Colonel John Belasyse's infantry brigade
G   Field artillery
H   Colonel Charles Gerard's cavalry brigade
I   Henry, Lord Wilmot's cavalry brigade
J   Prince Rupert's cavalry brigade
K   Colonel Robert Dormer, Earl of Carnarvon's cavalry brigade
L   Sir John Byron's cavalry brigade (part)

BATTLE OF NEWBURY

20 September 1643, viewed from the south-east. Prince Rupert makes a last bid to win the battle by driving a wedge between Skippon's and Essex's commands. The Blue and Red regiments of the London Trained Bands thwart his attempt.

Regiment to the right of the Red Regiment and farthest from the Royalist cannon. The Red Regiment bore the brunt of the artillery fire and Sergeant Foster recorded 'the enemie's cannon did play most against the red regiment of trained bands, they did some execution amongst us at the first, and were somewhat dreadfull when men's bowels and brains flew in our faces: But blessed be to God that gave us courage, so that we kept our ground, and after a while feared them not.'

The Trained Bands came under immediate heavy attack by 'two regiments of the kings horse which stood upon their right flank a far off, came fiercely upon them, two or three times, but were beat back by our muskettiers, who gave them a most desperate charge [volley], and made them flie'. Once Skippon could get his heavier artillery in place on the round hill he was able to support the Londoners and 'our ordnance did very good execution upon them [the Royalists], for we stood at such distance upon a plain field that we could not lightly misse one another'.

Under constant artillery fire, the Londoners joined their two regiments together into one body, fell back to a small hill and held out under new attacks from Royalist infantry and cavalry. Sergeant Foster recorded, 'two regiments of the enemie's foot fought against us all this while to gain the hill but could not. Then two regiments of the enemie's horse, which stood upon the right flank, came fiercely upon us, and so surrounded us, that wee were forced to charge upon them in front and reere, and both flanks.' 'Charge' in this sense is taken from the contemporary order to hold pikes in the drill position – 'charge your pike'. This meant that the London Trained Bands formed one large square, which was a contemporary defensive formation against cavalry, with their pikemen holding off Royalist cavalry on all sides. Forced back by another Royalist infantry attack, the Londoners fell back but rallied and advanced again. After over three hours of fighting the Royalists finally gave up on their attack on the London Trained Bands. Prince Rupert had lost his last opportunity to win the day. This was a truly remarkable defence, and an exceptional one as the Londoners were under prolonged and determined attack by foot, horse and artillery, and this should have been enough to beat any infantry formation, let alone militia who had not been in action before.

The Centre of the Battlefield

As the fighting continued amongst the banks and hedgerows in the centre, Skippon brought up the army's heavier artillery under Sir John Merrick to a position on the round hill. As the previous section and the Royalist accounts demonstrate, this position dominated the battlefield and provided essential support for the London Trained Bands. The Parliament artillery was supported by placing infantry formations on either side, a party of 'commanded' musketeers from Skippon's own regiment on the right and Red Auxiliaries on the left. Skippon retained the Orange Auxiliaries in hand as a final reserve.

The Northern Flank

The Parliament forces made demonstrations along this flank but probably without pressing too hard, as the main focus of their attention was in the centre and the south. The account of an unknown Royalist colonel recorded a stalemate in this area, 'In the meantime came Sir Lewis Kirke to mee with commands from ye King to goe looke to ye passe by the river

Pikemen were trained to use their weapons by repetitive practice in the optimum movements or 'postures'. The postures shown are 'Charge your Pike' and 'Charge for Horse'. Both sets of illustrations were based on an earlier Dutch original.

Charge your Pike.

side which the enemy were then endeavouring to gaine, but when I came to ye place I found Sir William Vavasour there with his brigade, which I conceived sufficiently secured that place.'

After the Battle

After hard fighting throughout the day the two sides had drawn apart by midnight. The Royalists had finally been successful in defeating the Parliament cavalry on the Southern flank, but they had gained no advantage from this as they had been unable to break the Parliament infantry anywhere on the battlefield. Essex's soldiers expected to have to renew the battle on the following day, but they remained in good spirits and were 'resolved by God's help the next day to force our way through them or dye'. However, the Royalists were now short of ammunition. The Oxford Royalist account recorded that 'having not (to tell you the truth) Powder enough left for halfe such another day, having spent four score barrels in it, three score more than had served the turne at Edgehill, nor could we be assured that the supply from Oxford of 100 Barrelles more could come to us till the next day at noon'.

Surviving Royalist Ordnance papers show that an urgent order was sent from camp near Newbury on 20 September to Sir John Heydon, Lieutenant General of the Ordnance, for 50 barrels of powder. The order was received at Oxford 'betweene 7 and 8 at night' and the urgency underlined by the annotation after receipt 'these things must needes goe away this night for Newburry'. The Royalist Ordnance office worked desperately hard and by 3 o'clock in the following morning 13 wagons and carts were despatched to Newbury carrying 50 barrels of powder, match and musket shot, and 'round shot of iron' for the King's artillery.

While the Royalists waited for fresh supplies of ammunition Essex's army were able to continue their march past Newbury as 'it pleased God to make our passage without blows; for the enemy was gone by night, so that the next morning we marched quietly over the same ground where the battail was fought.'

THE LONDON TRAINED BANDS FIGHTING OFF THE ROYALIST HORSE AT NEWBURY (pages 86–87)

By mid-afternoon a potential weak point was opening up between the Earl of Essex's men fighting in the open country to the south and Philip Skippon's force holding the enclosed ground in the centre and on the northern flank. Prince Rupert's Royalist force on the southern flank had finally been able to defeat the Earl of Essex's Parliament cavalry but had been unable to break the supporting infantry. Rupert now had one last chance to win the battle. If he could split the two sections of the Parliament army the Royalists could defeat each group separately. Prince Rupert had a combined force of infantry and cavalry and the support of the main Royalist artillery battery. Colonel Randall Mainwaring's, the first infantry regiment sent by Skippon to hold this ground, had been overwhelmed by a coordinated attack by Royalist cavalry and infantry. Skippon then sent two London Trained Bands regiments, the Red Regiment and the Blue Regiment, from his reserve to hold this position. These were militia regiments formed from London citizens. The London Trained Bands formed regimental squares and held out against a series of Royalist attacks. As the pressure increased the two regiments joined together to form one large body. Here we see one of these squares with two lines of musketeers kneeling in the front – the first line firing (1) and the second (2) reloading their matchlock muskets. Behind them stands the first line of pikemen (3) with the butts of their pikes set in the ground under their right foot with the head of the pike angled to the height of a horse's chest, a position called 'charge for horse'. Behind them stand further lines of pikemen (4) with their pikes charged horizontally. Both musketeers and pikemen wear their own civilian clothing under their military equipment, although the London musketeers were distinguished by the sleeveless buff coats they wore. They wear the Parliamentary field sign of the day, sprigs of furze (gorse) and broom, in their hats and helmets. Their equipment was privately purchased over a period of years and shows a range of different styles. The musketeers are using old-fashioned heavy muskets but cannot use their forked musket-rests when kneeling and have laid these on the ground beside them. The flag (5) seen in the background is the Sergeant-Major's flag of the Blue Regiment of the London Trained Bands. Each company in the regiment had its own flag and these are illustrated on pages 28 and 32–33. In the absence of their colonel, Lieutenant-Colonel Francis West commanded the Blue Regiment at Newbury with Sergeant-Major William Underwood as second in command. The Royalist cavalry (6) was unable to break the Londoners and could only fire their pistols and retire. This clash was a key moment in the war for until that point the Royalist cavalry had proved almost invincible, but the London Trained Bands more than held their own against the King's best troops. If the citizens of London would march so far from their homes in defence of Parliament's cause, 'with what success could his Majesty have approached London?' The capital was secure, her people committed to Parliament and the King's cavalry were no longer invincible – the balance of power had shifted irretrievably.

(Graham Turner)

AFTERMATH

THE MARCH HOME, 21–28 SEPTEMBER

Thursday 21 September

The author of the official Parliament account recorded that 'on Thursday early his Excellency gave command for the armie's march towards Reading, to which purpose it was all drawn up upon the heath where the battle was fought, and after his Excellency had given order for burying the dead, about ten of the clock we began to march.'

Essex had drawn up his army and offered battle, but the King's army lacked the ammunition to contest the field. Essex gave written orders to the churchwardens of the parish of Enbourne for the burial of 'all the dead bodies lying in and around Enbourne and Newbury Wash' and marched away from Newbury unopposed, carrying many of his wounded with him on his baggage wagons. The Parliament rearguard consisted of a brigade of cavalry under Colonel Middleton (his own regiment, Lord Grey's, James Sheffield's and Sir John Meldrum's regiments) and a 'Forlorn Hope' of 400 commanded musketeers under Colonel Barclay. The rearmost infantry formation was the City infantry brigade.

St Nicholas Church, Newbury. The churchwarden's accounts record expenses for 'burying dead soldiers in the Churchyard and the Wash [Wash Common]'.

Prince Rupert mounted a pursuit with the Royalist cavalry supported by Sir George Lisle's 'commanded' musketeers, now reduced to about 800 musketeers, and caught up with Essex's army during the late afternoon. Sergeant Foster recorded: 'in our march this day, our enemy pursuing of us, fell upon our reer [rearguard] in a narrow lane about a mile and a halfe from a village called Aldermason [Aldermaston]; they came upon us with a great body of foot and horse.' The Royalists overwhelmed Colonel Middleton's cavalry which 'durst [dared] not stand to charge the enemy, but fled, running into the narrow lane, routed our own foot, trampling many of them under their horse feet, crying out to them, "Away, away, every man shift for his life, you are all dead men" which caused a most strange confusion amongst us.'

The Parliament cavalry rode through Colonel Barclay's 'commanded' musketeers and carried them away in the rout. The rear of Essex's column was now in chaos: 'many of our waggons were overthrowne and broken: others cut their traces and horse-harnesse, and run away with their horses, leaving their waggons and carriages behind them.' The Royalist attack was checked as the rearmost Parliament infantry brigade, the London Trained Bands and Auxiliaries, deployed musketeers in the hedgerows and made use of their light artillery as Sergeant Foster recorded: 'We fired ten or twelve drakes at the enemy, but they came on very firecely having their foot on the other side of the hedges.'

The London soldiers were initially forced back but they rallied and 'fired upon the enemie's horse very bravely, and slew many of them, some report above a hundred and not ten of ours; some that we took prisoners

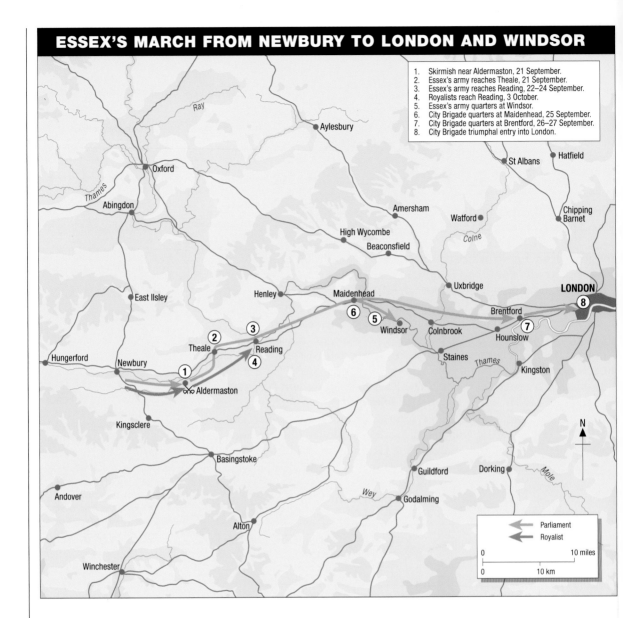

1. Skirmish near Aldermaston, 21 September.
2. Essex's army reaches Theale, 21 September.
3. Essex's army reaches Reading, 22–24 September.
4. Royalists reach Reading, 3 October.
5. Essex's army quarters at Windsor.
6. City Brigade quarters at Maidenhead, 25 September.
7. City Brigade quarters at Brentford, 26–27 September.
8. City Brigade triumphal entry into London.

Parliament
Royalist

0   10 miles

0   10 km

our men were so inraged at them that they knockt out their braines with the butt end of their muskets. In this great distraction and rout a waggon of powder lying the way overthrowne, some spark of fire or match fell among it, which did much hurt; seven men burnt and two kill'd: the enemy had got two of our drakes in the reer, had not our foot played the men and recovered them againe: this was about four or five o'clock.'

Having fought off Prince Rupert's attack Essex's army crossed the River Kennet at Padworth and then 'marched on and came to the Veal [Theale] about ten o'clock at night'.

Friday 22–Sunday 24 September

Essex 'marched next morning being Friday with the whole army to Reading, where we stayed till the sabbath was past, and gave publique thanks for the great victory … [at Reading] we refreshed our souldiers after our hard service and wearisome marchings. We stayed here Fryday,

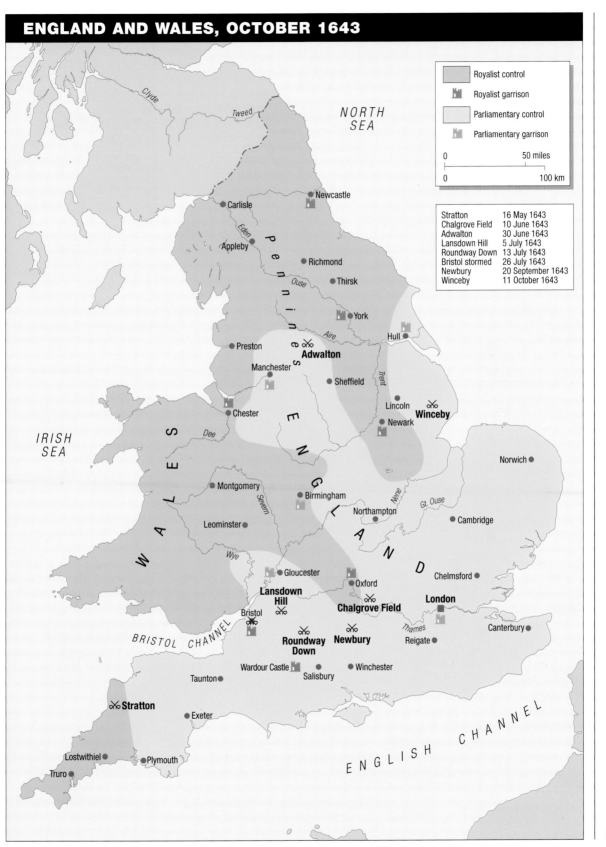

ENGLAND AND WALES, OCTOBER 1643

NORTH
SEA

IRISH
SEA

BRISTOL CHANNEL

ENGLISH CHANNEL

WALES

ENGLAND

Pennines

Clyde
Tweed
Eden
Ouse
Aire
Trent
Nene
Gt. Ouse
Dee
Severn
Wye
Thames

Newcastle
Carlisle
Appleby
Richmond
Thirsk
York
Preston
Adwalton
Manchester
Sheffield
Hull
Lincoln
Winceby
Chester
Newark
Norwich
Montgomery
Birmingham
Leominster
Northampton
Cambridge
Gloucester
Oxford
Chelmsford
Lansdown Hill
Chalgrove Field
London
Bristol
Canterbury
Roundway Down
Newbury
Reigate
Wardour Castle
Winchester
Taunton
Salisbury
Stratton
Exeter
Lostwithiel
Plymouth
Truro

Royalist control
Royalist garrison
Parliamentary control
Parliamentary garrison

0   50 miles
0   100 km

Stratton	16 May 1643
Chalgrove Field	10 June 1643
Adwalton	30 June 1643
Lansdown Hill	5 July 1643
Roundway Down	13 July 1643
Bristol stormed	26 July 1643
Newbury	20 September 1643
Winceby	11 October 1643

Saterday, and sabbath day: Saterday night about twenty of the enemie's horse came and gave us an alarm. Sabbath day was celebrated a day of thanksgiving; we marched away hence on Munday morning [25 September].'

Monday 25 September

Essex 'having left the greatest part of his Forces at Reading, and the parts adjacent' returned to London ahead of them 'which was on Munday the 25'.

Tuesday 26 September

On the afternoon of 26 September Essex and 'divers of the Lords in Parliament, and of the House of Commons with their Speaker went into Finsbury Fields' to view a muster of the remaining London Trained Bands and Auxiliary regiments (the thirteen regiments which had remained behind during this campaign). At the end of the muster each regiment 'by their loud acclamations testified their great affection for his excellency and each regiment as he [Essex] passed by, gave him a volley of shot with Collours displayed in a very exact manner.' This was a significant event as it showed that the City Militia regiments, encouraged by accounts of the prowess of the City regiments that had fought at Newbury, were solidly behind the Earl of Essex and the Parliament cause.

Thursday 28 September

Essex did not try to hold Reading. His army retired on his garrison at Windsor, and the London Militia regiments returned to a heroes' welcome in the capital. 'On Thursday, the 28 September 1643, the Lord Mayor, Aldermen, Sheriffs, and Common Council, with divers other able and worthy citizens, rode on horseback out of the City to meet them on their return, thereby testifying their great affection unto them, for their great courage and valour in the cause of God and his people.' The London newsbook the *Parliament Scout* also records the return of the City forces on 28 September, stating they 'went through the City with green boughs in their hats in signall of victory'.

THE LAST WORD

After the battle of Newbury, different factions amongst the Royalists in Oxford bickered over where responsibility lay for their failure. Clarendon's summary was that 'upon the King's return to Oxford, there appeared nothing but dejection of mind, discontent, and secret mutiny; in the army, anger and jealousy amongst the officers, every one accusing another of want of courage and conduct in the actions of the field; and they were not of the army, blaming them all for their several failings and gross oversight.'

By contrast, in London there was celebration and the sense that military success showed that God was on their side. Sergeant Foster's summary was that, 'God called us forth to doe his worke, brought us through many straits, delivered us from the rage and insolency of our adversaries, made them turn their backes with shame, giving us victory, and causing us to returne home joyfully'.

The Victorian historian Walter Money organised a collection to raise this monument to those who fell at Newbury. There are inscriptions on each of the four sides. The main inscription reads, 'In memory of those who, on the 20th September, 1643 fell fighting in the army of Charles I, on the field of Newbury, and especially Lucius Cary, Viscount Falkland who died here in the 34th year of his age. This monument is set up by those to whom the Majesty of the Crown and the Liberties of their Country are dear.'

Donnington Castle. The Royalists garrisoned the castle after the battle of Newbury. The commission appointing the governor, Sir John Boys, is dated 22 September 1643.

For all practical purposes the Parliament's financial and military base at London was now impregnable and, with their failure at the siege of Gloucester and the battle of Newbury, the high point of Royalist military superiority had passed. When Essex's army marched out on this risky expedition the Royalist cause was in the ascendant. When he returned to London, the Parliament cause was revitalised and his opponents were despondent. In the spring of 1643 the King held the upper hand in the war, but failure to prevent the relief of Gloucester or block Essex's march home at Newbury broke this pattern and the battle of Newbury was the turning point of the English Civil War.

The Parliament colonels whose account was printed in London as 'the late expedition for the relief of Gloucester' sought to inform their readers as their opening comments set out: 'Thus gentle reader, hast thou had a description of the whole expedition in a narration plain and particular, if too much particularity have not made it tedious, and perplext both the stile and thy patience.' But their account also contains the most evocative 'last word' for 1643 as they concluded with the comment that Essex 'was heartily sorry for the losse of so many gallant gentlemen on their [the Royalist] side. Which (without jesting) I dare sweare he is; since there is no victory in civill warre that can bring the conquerer a perfect triumph.'

By 1643 both sides could see all too well that everyone loses something in a civil war, but that is not the same as to suggest that neither side thought they could win. There may not be a 'perfect triumph' in civil war, but both sides still sought to end the war by military victory. As the campaign season drew to a close both sides began to consider their strategies for new campaigns in 1644.

THE BATTLEFIELD TODAY

There are two places to visit during a tour of Newbury. The battlefield itself and the museum, which forms part of the Tourist Information Centre.

Newbury can be reached by following the M4 to Junction 13 and from there taking the A339 south to Newbury. At this point the visitor has the option of visiting the museum first or the battlefield itself. To view the battlefield follow the A343 out of Newbury to the junction where the Falkland Monument can easily be seen. This places the visitor in the centre of the battlefield looking west towards the feature described in Royalist accounts as the 'round hill'.

Thirsty or hungry visitors will find *The Gun* public house immediately opposite the Falkland monument. The last historian to write on the battles of Newbury, Walter Money in 1881, noted the position of this public house in his map of the battlefield. So the essential elements of historical research have not changed.

The town of Newbury expanded considerably during the 20th century. The site of the Royalist positions in front of Newbury and on Wash Common to the South have now been built over. However, the Parliament battle lines can still be seen and it is still possible to gain an impression of the terrain.

The museum has a small exhibition of artefacts relating to the battle, including some items recovered from the battlefield.

BIBLIOGRAPHY

Main Contemporary Accounts

Bibliotheca Gloucestrensis: A collection of scarce and curious tracts relating to the County and City of Gloucester, Parts I–II (Gloucester and London, 1823)

John Corbet, *An Historical Relation of the Military Government of Gloucester* (London, 1645)

John Dorney, *A briefe and exact relation of the most materiall and remarkable passages that happened in the late well-formed (and as valiantly defended) siege laid before the City of Gloucester collected by John Dorney, Esquire, Town-Clarke of the said City* (London, 1643)

Henry Foster, a sergeant in the London Militia., *A True and Exact Relation of the Marchings of the Two Regiments of the Trained Bands of the City of London* (London, 1643)

Account by Parliament Colonels, *A True Relation of the Late Expedition of His Excellency, Robert Earle of Essex, for the Relief of Gloucester* (London, 1643)

Sir John Byron (Royalist), MS account of the battles of Newbury in a letter to Clarendon by Sir John Byron. Add Ms 1738, Clarendon State Papers, Bodleian Library (written circa 1647)

From a letter by the Royalist Lord Digby, *A True and Impartial Relation of the Battaile betwixt His Majesties Army and that of the Rebells neare Newbury in Berkshire* (Oxford, 1643)

Unknown Royalist officer., MS account by an unknown Royalist officer. British Library Add MS 18980

Parliament Weekly Newsbooks, (1) A Continuation of Certain Speciall and Remarkable Passages, (2) Mercurius Britannicus, (3) Mercurius Civicus, (4) The *Parliament Scout*, (5) A Perfect Diurnall of some Passages in Parliament, (6) The True Informer, (7) The Weekly Account

Royalist Weekly Newsbook, *Mercurius Aulicus*

The Earl of Clarendon, *The History of the Rebellion and Civil Wars in England* (Oxford, Clarendon Press, 1888)

Secondary Sources

Malcolm Atkin and Wayne Laughlin, *Gloucester and the Civil War, A City under Siege* (Alan Sutton Publishing, 1992)

David Frampton and Peter Garnham, *The Forlorn Hope Guide to the First Battle of Newbury 1643* (Partizan Press 1997).

S.R. Gardiner, *History of the Great Civil War*, 4 vols 1642 to 1649 (Longmans, Green & Co, 1893)

W. Money, *Battles of Newbury* (Second edition, London, 1884)

Robert Morris, *The First Battle of Newbury 1643* (Stuart Press, 1993)

Stuart Peachey and Alan Turton, *Old Robin's Foot, the equipping and campaigns of Essex's infantry 1642–1645* (Partizan Press, 1987)

Stuart Reid, *War in the West, part 1, The Fall of the West* (Stuart Press, 1994)

Keith Roberts, *London & Liberty, Ensigns of the London Trained Bands* (Partizan Press, 1987)

Dr Ian Roy, *The Royalist Ordnance Paper, 1642–1646,* Parts I and II (Oxfordshire Record Society, 1964 and 1975)

Norman Tucker (ed), *Military Memoirs: The Civil War* (John Gwyn) (Longmans, Green & Co, 1967)

Alan Turton, *The Chief Strength of the Army, Essex's Horse (1642–1645)* (Partizan Press, 1992)

English Civil War Notes & Queries, See issues 10, 11, 19, 27 and 29 for articles on regiments which fought at Newbury

INDEX